Kevin B. Bucknall's
Cultural Guide to Doing Business in China

*To Sieska, who improved
the quality of my life*

Kevin B. Bucknall's Cultural Guide to Doing Business in China

Kevin B. Bucknall

BUTTERWORTH
HEINEMANN

Butterworth-Heinemann Ltd
Linacre House, Jordan Hill, Oxford OX2 8DP

ᴿ A member of the Reed Elsevier plc group

OXFORD   LONDON   BOSTON
MUNICH   NEW DELHI   SINGAPORE   SYDNEY
TOKYO   TORONTO   WELLINGTON

First published 1994

© Kevin B. Bucknall 1994

British Library Cataloguing in Publication Data
Bucknall, Kevin B.
   Kevin B. Bucknall's Cultural Guide to
   Doing Business in China
   I. Title
   382.0951

ISBN 0 7506 1983 X

Typeset by Scribe Design, Gillingham, Kent
Printed in Great Britain by Clays, St Ives plc

Contents

Preface   vii

Introduction   1

Part One   Appropriate Behaviour or What to Do

1   General points on proper behaviour   25
2   Approaching China   43
     Who to send   45
3   Meetings and negotiations   50
     Early meetings   52
4   Meetings and negotiations – your tactics   61
5   Meetings and negotiations – their tactics   72
     Contracts   78
6   Socializing and proper behaviour   84
7   How to treat visitors to one's own country   90
8   Living in China   93
     Establish the ground rules before departure   99
9   Managing joint ventures   102
     Labour and incentives   105

Part Two   Inappropriate Behaviour or What Not To Do

10   General points on proper behaviour   111
11   Approaching China   120
12   Meetings and negotiations   122
13   Socializing and proper behaviour   132
14   Living and managing in China   135
15   How to treat visitors to one's own country   139

Part Three   Summary of What to Do

16   General points on proper behaviour   143

17 Approaching China   145
    Who to send   145
18 Meetings and negotiations   146
    Early meetings   146
19 Meetings and negotiations – your tactics   148
20 Meetings and negotiations – their tactics   149
    Contracts   149
21 Socializing and proper behaviour   151
22 How to treat visitors to one's own country   152
23 Living in China   153
    Establish the ground rules before departure   153
24 Managing joint ventures   154
    Labour and incentives   154

Part Four Summary of What Not to Do

25 General points on proper behaviour   157
26 Approaching China   159
27 Meetings and negotiations   160
28 Socializing and proper behaviour   162
29 Living and managing in China   163
30 How to treat visitors to one's own country   164

Index   165

Preface

This book is intended to make you and your company or government department more successful when dealing with foreign institutions. Cultures are very different from each other; what is normal and acceptable in one can easily be extremely offensive in another. Most people learn about the basic good manners and standard acceptable behaviour when very young and are taught by their parents, especially their mother. Other good manners are picked up by observation and perhaps by reading magazine articles or books on etiquette, etc. The problem with visiting another culture as an adult is that no one informs you of such things and virtually everyone is too embarrassed to tell you about your unacceptable behaviour. As a result, it is easy to visit a foreign country, or even spend many years living there, and unknowingly give offence.

As a business person or government official, it is easy to insult someone who may already not be particularly fond of foreigners generally, or who may even have a grudge against your country for real or imagined historical or contemporary political reasons. Your normal polite behaviour can easily inadvertently lose you a sale or contract, or prevent the signing of an official agreement, and you may never understand why. In the area of table manners, actions such as slurping tea or soup are quite acceptable in some societies but are regarded as disgusting in others. Even the colours you wear or the way you sit can offend in some countries.

The information provided here is intended to be used when visiting a foreign country and dealing with the inhabitants. The focus is on the things to do and to avoid doing in order to prevent giving offence and also to demonstrate your sensitivity and understanding of the country. Naturally, it is equally valuable when you deal with foreign business people or government officials who are visiting your country. By following the suggestions you should be able to improve your image, achieve greater success in negotiations, sell more, make higher profits, sign more agreements and generally better achieve whatever is your aim. At the very least, you will give yourself an edge on your competitors. It may not be necessary to memorize all the points as they can be quickly looked up, nor need you follow all of them scrupulously. However, the more you can use, the better you will be able to function.

Most existing books on doing business with people from other cultures fall into one of two groups. The first kind is often written by a business person who has learned practical things about doing business in a particular country, sometimes laboriously over several years, and is passing on the fruits of wisdom, often with many anecdotes. While intrinsically interesting, such books tend to be limited by the kind of business done, and the anecdotes are often only of use when the circumstances you will face are very similar. It is therefore often not easy to apply the lessons from the 'this happened to me' school of business advice.

The second kind of book is more academic, and is frequently designed for use in a course such as an MA in Business Administration. Much space is usually devoted to case studies. These are often intended for group discussion and rarely do they supply anything like a complete explanation of what was well done or what went wrong. In some cases they supply no 'answers' at all, as they rely on group discussions to ferret out solutions and suggestions. In most cases their value is to sensitize the reader to problems of cross-cultural communication, but such books may not be of great practical assistance, especially to a lone business person or government official.

This book is different from both the above types. The information is practical and provided in a brief, simple and direct way which can easily be used. Few busy people, in business or government, have the time to read copiously about each country with which they may have to deal, and such practical information as might be useful is often in obscure journals or buried in books. Apart from providing an under-standing of the culture of China and demonstrating how you can most easily operate within it, realistic advice is given on how to improve your negotiating skills and how the Chinese team may be expected to operate.

The ways to behave for increased success are explained in the context of Chinese culture, separated into practical sections concerned with how to approach China, meetings and negotiations, socializing, treating Chinese visitors to your country, living in China and manag-ing joint ventures. Each point is numbered for convenience. The book starts with the things you should do for increased success, then discusses those you should avoid doing. The individual points are then summarized like a shopping list, which makes the information very accessible. For example, you may wish to remind yourself of points of good behaviour or negotiating tactics while on an aircraft or even in a taxi on the way to a meeting. The information in point form can also be memorized if you so wish. You will find it easy to move back from a particular summary point to read the more detailed explanation as the note numbers are the same.

You may think that it is unnecessary to bother to learn about another nation's habits, customs and manners and feel that the other people should accept yours. Alternatively, you may feel that what has worked successfully for you in your country will do so when dealing with others, and that what is considered to be good manners in your country is sufficient anywhere. Perhaps you feel that you should not change a winning formula. Some people feel this way, but they are unlikely to win friends and influence people in other countries, and the practical results in terms of sales or trade agreements signed quickly are likely to be slimmer. Remember that you do not negate or reject your own culture by learning about someone else's. Nor is it obsequious or fawning to learn about and not violate the values of others. True, it would be easier for you if foreigners learned your values and adopted them, but we must remember that we are all foreigners once we leave the boundaries of our own country. The question is, are you prepared to learn and adapt your behaviour in order to avoid offending your counterparts and customers and those with whom you negotiate, or are you not? If you avoid giving offence it can only work for the good of your firm, country and career. It is clearly to your advantage to avoid offence but the choice in the end must be yours. The information in this book will help you to make the necessary changes if you are willing to learn.

While we believe that the information provided is the best currently available, you should be aware that societies change, although culture does this more slowly than some facets of a nation, such as which are the best restaurants. These changes mean that a suggestion can slowly become less useful, especially when dealing with the younger generation. Many of the countries of East and South-east Asia in particular are undergoing rapid economic growth which is placing pressure on traditional values and practices. We would be delighted to hear from you if you find any points that could be improved, or your experience reveals new points that can be added. Please address any suggestions for improvement to the author, care of the publisher.

Two final words of caution are necessary. First, you should beware of treating all Chinese as stereotypes who will always behave as described below. People are individuals and should be treated as such, even though they all operate within the confines of their culture. You will find that not everyone you meet in a foreign country conforms exactly to the prevailing culture, just as not all people do in your society. Some people do not know how to behave and others simply do not care. However, one tends to find relatively few successful business people or public officials who behave in ways considered to be actually offensive in their own country. If you see behaviour in China that appears to conflict with the cultural norms described here, you can flatter yourself that you are able to recognize this fact. The do's and don'ts suggested here refer to the generally accepted rules of behaviour that should stand you in good stead.

Second, being adept at cross-cultural communication is extremely valuable but it is not enough to solve all your problems. It is a supplement to other skills, not a replacement. You still need to be an experienced skilful manager, used to negotiating and relating to people, making good decisions, putting together deals and devising alternatives. What you learn here will help you to function more effectively when dealing with the Chinese but is is not a substitute for other management skills.

Kevin B. Bucknall

Introduction

History

The oldest Chinese books still in existence date back to almost 1000 BC, although various myths and legends, as well as archeological evidence including samples of early writing, suggest there was an even earlier period. China has the longest continuous history and culture of any currently existing nation. The Chinese are a proud people, with more awareness of the past than most Westerners. Events that occurred a thousand or more years ago are well known to educated people and stories and legends abound. References to ancient events and long dead people are common in contemporary discussion and there is a tendency to look back on history to gain lessons of value for the present. In both the past and present this provides scope for plays and stories, ostensibly about the past, which actually criticize current leaders and policies.

China was a stable empire for two thousand years, in the hands of a series of ruling dynasties. This system only collapsed in 1911 with the passing of the Manchu Dynasty. Its decline was hastened by the impact of the West, especially by Britain, during the colonial expansions of the nineteenth century. The First Opium War of 1839–42 had a traumatic effect on Chinese leaders, who began an intense search for the best way to organize China to meet these new and powerful barbarians. After the fall of the imperial dynasty, there was a brief flirtation with an embryo type of parliamentary democracy. This lasted for less than two years before President Yuan Shihkai seized total control; he did not last long either and after his unsuccessful attempt to establish a new dynasty, China collapsed into warlordism as the nation fell apart. After 1916, many independent little 'kingdoms' were established, banditry was rife, and in 1928 civil war broke out between the Kuomintang (KMT) and the communists, which divided the country. In 1931 the Japanese invaded China and rapidly took over control of all the important areas. Sucked into the Second World War by the presence of the Japanese, at the end of hostilities China was given back to the KMT. The civil war was rapidly resumed in 1946 and ended in 1949 with victory to the communists. In that year, the KMT moved its seat of government to the island of Taiwan, from where it claimed still to be the legitimate ruler of all China. At least nominally the civil war continues unresolved, although there has been no military action for years and both governments began to talk almost officially in Singapore in 1993. There has been a notable economic rapprochement during the 1990s, based on China's need for foreign investment and technology and Taiwan's need for cheap labour. The inhabitants of both areas accept the strong bond of ethnicity, despite major political differences. Direct China–Taiwan foreign trade is still banned by Taiwan, but indirect trade is now commonplace, largely via Hong Kong. Much foreign investment flows from Taiwan to China; estimates suggest that around US$8 billion has been committed so far.

The political scene

China enjoys a government by geriatrics; youth is generally mistrusted, especially with power. No one under thirty years of age is regarded as being mature and few under fifty exercise much authority at higher levels of government. Since 1949 anyone who took part in the famous 'Long March' (1934–35), when the beleaguered communist forces trekked 10,000 km across China to a safe haven in Yennan in the North-West, had immense power and was virtually untouchable, however poor their performance. With the passing of time, few are now left, but even being related to such a person can bring social status and perhaps some local power.

China is an authoritarian, one-party state, under the control of the Chinese Communist Party (CCP). A handful of unimportant non-Communist parties are allowed to exist and have grown in importance in recent years. This means they have changed from possessing no power at all to having an insignificant amount. The CCP is the executive power in the land, and has mostly been run by a single person with immense control: in effect this makes him a dictator. For a time during the Cultural Revolution (1966–76) Mao Zedong's wife, Chiang Ching, exercised much power, but as one of the Gang of Four she was eclipsed shortly after the death of Mao in 1976. Other than that, China has been male-dominated since 1911.

At the political centre of things there is a Central Committee, which controls everything, under the supreme leader. It is at the level of this Central Committee that power can pass from one leader to another, particularly in the small Standing Committee of the Central Committee. Unlike the full Central Committee which gets together only occasionally, the Standing Committee meets regularly and is something like a Cabinet in Western terms.

The legislative power in China is the National People's Congress (NPC) which until recently has been a lap dog totally under the control of the CCP. During the 1980s it began to assert itself in minor ways, which may seem striking to the Chinese and many foreign observers, but the NPC is hardly an independent body and cannot be regarded as possessing the power of an ordinary Western Parliament. Despite occasional (and well-publicized) critical speeches, the CCP is still able to dominate it without any worries about real opposition.

China is divided administratively into twenty-nine bodies of provincial status, including a few Autonomous Regions and Direct Run Cities. Each of these levels has its own government. Below these are more than 2000 counties, and various towns, each with its own local government. Because China is so vast, much power has to be decentralized to local levels and this is where many important decisions are made, not always in line with central policy, or indeed legally.

Since December 1978 the CCP has been engaged in a major effort to resuscitate and improve the economy. That was the year that Deng Xiaoping finally got the numbers in the CCP and gained control after two years of intra-party struggles. These had surfaced immediately after the death of Chairman Mao Zedong in September 1976 and involved two issues: who should run China and along what policy lines. After the demise of Mao, the country had an inefficient moribund economy, a people wearied of political unheaval and change, and numbers of vocal and enthusiastic supporters of Maoism. If economic progress was to be made, this situation had to be altered. Deng Xiaoping set about doing so, cautiously at first and then with increasing speed as the reforms took root.

The CCP itself is divided into three very loose factions: reformist marketeers (loosely Titoists), traditional die-hard communists (loosely Stalinists) and radical Maoist revolutionaries. The philosophies and preferred methods of these factions differ so markedly it may be hard for some casual observers to accept that they are in the same Party. The marketeers, led by Deng Xiaoping, gained power in 1978 and have retained it since. There is lack of unity even within this group as to how far reliance should be placed on use of the market; there is a pragmatic wing, led by Deng Xiaoping, which is strongly in favour of the market; and there is a more conservative wing, which believes in allowing restricted use of the market mainly in order to improve the workings of central planning. All political changes since 1979 seem to reflect a swing between the relative power of these two reformist wings within the marketeers' camp. Although not a lot is known about the inner workings of Chinese politics, it would seem that each of the three main political groupings in China contains differing factions and the situation is quite fluid as people switch factions and relative power alters.

The overall policy of the current leaders of China can reasonably accurately be described as 'Communism with an acceptable capitalist face', although the official version is 'A socialist market economy with Chinese characteristics'. The socialist market economy was written into the Constitution of China in 1993 by a series of amendments. The current Constitution, the fourth since 1949, was adopted in 1982. Any really major political change eventually leads to the promulgation of a new Constitution. The general thrust of policy since 1978 has been to reform a moribund economy while maintaining the political power monopoly of the Communist Party. There is currently no intention of the leadership to move towards a Western democratic system.

In more precise terms, domestic political policy since 1978 has included the following.

1   To end Maoism and remove all strong Maoist sympathizers from positions of power.
2   To replace such people with pro-market sympathizers and thereby reinforce the position of the ruling faction.
3   To prevent the Stalinists from regaining control within the Party.
4   To keep the CCP in power as the process of reforming the economy proceeds.
5   To keep the People's Liberation Army (PLA) on side with the pro-market faction and use them both to support the reformers and to maintain civil order and control. This includes holding China together and avoiding any danger of provinces splitting away or China falling into civil war.

The country has traditionally been difficult to hold together because of its size; typically it has started to disintegrate as the ruling dynasty weakened and has then been pulled together again by strong central leadership under a new dynasty. The current leadership, well aware of this pattern, is striving to prevent this traditional process from getting under way. This is one reason they were prepared to get tough in Tiananmen Square in June 1989 and send in the army.

These political aims have been successfully achieved. Domestically, the Maoists have been whittled away until on the surface there appear to be none left. Underneath the political surface they are thought to continue to exist but, lacking any real power base, they currently show no sign of resurgence. The Stalinists are thought to be well outnumbered, but remain hopeful and have a few powerful backers in the Party. There is no sign that the pro-market leadership faction is going to lose power in the near future.

Politically there has been little fundamental change: the Communist Party is still in charge and allows no serious opposition, although its own power and stature have diminished. The general intention to keep the CCP in power during the period of economic reform has also been successfully achieved. This is particularly so when compared with the situation in East Europe and particularly the former Yugoslavia or USSR. In China the state has been maintained, civil war avoided, the Party retains power and the political decision-making process is neither chaotic nor paralysed. Firm control has been maintained, even as the shackles on freedom have been slackened to a significant extent.

The movement towards increased use of the market has been relatively slow and careful; often the rulers slackened power a little, watched the results carefully, then adopted as official policy what was actually being successfully done at grass root levels. Sometimes different things were tried out in different areas, the results compared and the best methods selected. This bottom-up pragmatism has meant that policies have been appropriate to the situation faced, rather than being imposed from above and hence possibly unsuitable.

The PLA has supported the ruling reformist branch of the CCP and even intervened in the Tiananmen Massacre on 4 June 1989 to put down the students and workers and maintain the status quo. What is referred to in China as 'The Tiananmen Incident' was a major setback to a small group of people in China who wanted the establishment of something like a Western democracy and to a larger group of more general supporters. Many people, especially in urban China, were antagonized by some features that accompanied the reform of the economy. These included corruption, inflation, a rise in the level of uncertainty and a diminution of the standards of public and private morality generally. Those involved in the demonstrations in Tiananmen Square were often students, accompanied by some workers, especially journalists. Some of the demonstrators were protesting against the above unwanted features of reform; others simply wanted a bit more freedom; and a few others probably did not know what they wanted, other than a change of some kind. The end result, when the army went in with its tanks, was to squash the hopes of a relatively limited number of Chinese, especially among the educated and literate, roughly equivalent to those often referred to in Britain as 'the chattering classes'. There is probably more concern abroad than in China and the Tiananmen episode antagonized many foreign observers. The latter tend to identify with both Western values and middle-class aspirations. The vast majority of Chinese are peasants and were uninvolved in any of the furore. In poor areas their horizons tend to be limited to survival; in better areas to economic gain or even getting rich. Their interest in politics does not seem to loom large.

In practical terms, the Tiananmen massacre caused few economic losses and these were short-lived. Economic growth rapidly resumed, the minimal sanctions imposed by foreign countries were soon abandoned and the foreign tourists quickly returned. By 1991 the number of tourists and foreign exchange earned from them exceeded the pre-Tiananmen levels. Foreign investment also recommenced and indeed increased so rapidly that in 1993 China overtook Mexico to become the largest recipient of foreign direct investment in the world.

The PLA, once a Maoist stronghold, was previously trained to fight guerrilla wars, with little modern equipment. It now has a brand new role (to maintain civil order and to become a more modern Western-style army) and has been slightly modernized. Its equipment and training lag well behind its new role, because China is too poor to put sufficient resources into defence, despite increases in the defence budget since the late 1980s. The PLA operates many farms and factories and sells about two-thirds of its industrial output to civilians, but is still short of money for the needed modernization.

Since 1978, China's policies at the international level have been to move China back into the world and increase the number of friendly nations, while developing foreign trade and foreign investment in China. In the longer term, it is to make China globally a great nation. Precise goals have included reducing tension with Vietnam, removing the wide political gap between China and South Korea and moving closer towards Taiwan. The collapse of the Soviet Union fortuitously removed an enemy for China – the earlier border disputes as well as major ideological differences had previously put them seriously at odds with one another.

These international aims have been achieved and South Korea is now an important trade partner of China and a source of foreign investment. Taiwan and China, both still insisting that there is only one government of China, have begun to talk openly as well as engage in trade. Taiwanese firms also invest in China and *de facto* there are two political states, although the concept of 'two Chinas' is a prickly one that neither China nor Taiwan will accept. China never refers to Taiwan as a 'country'.

In addition, the future of the two Western colonies, Hong Kong and Macao, has been successfully negotiated and both will revert to China (Hong Kong at midnight on 30 June 1997 and Macao on 20 December 1999) to be run as Special Administrative Regions of China. For China's sake, the process of transition of these two areas should be as smooth as possible. This is a major reason why in December 1993 China strongly objected to the introduction of a degree of Western-style democracy in Hong Kong. China sees the issue as a blatant attempt to limit China's sovereignty in the future and an exercise in cynical political manoeuvring by Britain. China points out that democracy was a feature that Britain was more than happy to do without as long as it had sole responsibility for the territory. Britain sees the issue as a way of increasing the guarantee that China will abide by the agreement on Hong Kong, and in particular to avoid any major changes for fifty years.

A further part of China's international policies has been to develop and increase international respect for China, maintain political independence and prevent any interference in China's domestic affairs. The issue of civil rights for Chinese citizens, including in minority areas such as Tibet, falls in this area. The aims of respect and independence have been successfully met, but civil rights, especially in Tibet, remain an issue for which China is regularly criticized abroad. The USA in particular tends to do this on an annual basis. Each year, Congress votes on the issue of whether to extend m.f.n. treatment to China and critics take advantage of the occasion to raise anything of concern. These are usually in the area of human rights. The Chinese, who are a proud people with an immensely long recorded history and culture, do not take kindly to this process of foreign criticism. It is resented as being an open interference in the internal affairs of China.

In 1988, China applied for readmission to GATT, but the discussions about conditions for entry have still not been concluded. It will not be an easy task, for although China's economy has been greatly reformed, it is still far from being a free one and many market restrictions continue. These include quotas and licences, some high tariffs, much arbitrary official interference and the existence of secret, unpublished regulations. None of these are compatible with GATT membership. As China continues to reduce its reliance on administrative controls it should find GATT readmission easier. On the issue of Taiwan, China is prepared to allow it to join GATT, but sit as a separate customs area of China, not as a country.

The economic scene

Between the early 1950s and the late 1970s, China put in place and ran a ramshackle planned economy. Although total planning of the economy was intended, this was never really achieved. The task was too immense in such a vast country, with its problems of communications and transport, shortage of skills and record of regular political interference. During the Cultural Revolution (1966–76), radical political rectitude replaced economic progress as a goal. At the death of Chairman Mao (1976) the economy was in a poor state. As a result of political extremism the people had learned that it was dangerous to succeed economically and make progress. This attitude was inimical to economic growth. In addition, the statistical reporting system was in tatters and no one knew much about the real situation anywhere. Resources had been grossly misallocated for years, and agriculture in particular had been starved of financial investment, so that no modernization had occurred there. Labour intensive methods were used by hundreds of millions of peasants organized in communes, production brigades and production teams. In industry, workers had been demoralized and the once proud work ethic of the Chinese had been eroded or in many cases totally removed. Such economic growth as had occurred had been uncontrolled, with the result that good agricultural land had been lost to cultivation, while air and water pollution had become a serious problem.

The issue of the economy had to be tackled, especially as the population had increased considerably – by 1976 it was 73 per cent above the size of 1949, but despite well-publicized land reclamation, the amount of arable land available had barely increased – the result of inroads by industrialization and urbanization. The lack of attention to economic matters after 1966, despite valiant efforts by Premier Zhou Enlai, who did his best against long political odds and in later years a doddering and vindictive Mao, meant that by 1976 no one even knew much about what had actually happened in the economy or what resources were available. Something had to be done. A two-year survey was held in order to see what China had available to use. As information trickled in, a grandiose ten-year plan was approved in March 1978, but this was rapidly abandoned in December, even before it had begun. Political change had rendered it instantly obsolete.

Socially, by the death of Mao, the Chinese people were ready for a change: they had suffered too much. They were tired of the political terror, the all-pervading influence of radical politics on every detail of ordinary life, and they wanted peace. A return to normality was clearly needed. It was, however, unclear who was to supply this, or indeed what normality meant. For many it meant a return to Soviet-style communism, with five-year and annual plans within a regime of command economy and the reinstitution of a rather grey, bureaucratic, dull but predictable situation. Such a group, under Hua Guofeng, seized the reins of power 1976–78, but soon lost them to Deng Xiaoping and his followers, who had a very different answer to the problems of the lacklustre economy.

In late 1978 Deng's group, who had taken over the Party leadership, began to allow some relaxation of the commitment to central planning and permitted some, if minimal, use of the market. This was deliberately engineered from above, although it rapidly got out of hand and gained a momentum of its own. The process began on a limited scale in agriculture and before long it led to the disbanding of communes and the introduction of private farming on what was nominally state-owned land. Efforts to introduce private methods in state-run industry were not particularly successful for a long time, but shares in some state-owned enterprises were sold. A primitive capital market has been established, with limited stock markets set up in Shanghai and Shenzhen Special Economic Zone (SEZ), on which selected companies are allowed to be listed. Currently these number about seventy. Other large state firms have been broken up and their monopoly positions removed. The state airline, CAAC, suffered this fate and the small remaining portion faces competition from a variety of regional firms. In industry generally, privately-run firms are now allowed and these have mushroomed in recent years.

Wholesale markets did not exist until recently, as there was no need for them under central planning. Several such markets were established in the early 1990s, covering commodities such as timber, building materials, farm machinery, coal, petroleum and metals. In 1993 the Shanghai Metals Exchange became the third largest in the world after London and Chicago. The previously ludicrously low prices for capital goods and basic raw materials have begun to increase and, although still low, are moving towards international levels. China expects to have an efficient market distribution system for all such types of goods by the end of the century.

A few steps along the way to establishing a labour market have been taken. No longer are the children of all peasants doomed to be peasants in their turn, nor are the offspring of all workers allocated to jobs on a rather ad hoc and inefficient basis by the state. Youngsters are no longer forced to 'wait for employment', a euphemism which meant that they were really unemployed but not counted in the figures nor allowed to describe themselves as such. Peasants now have more freedom to move and workers can themselves apply for jobs rather than be forced to wait until allocated one. They can also move to seek work for themselves, more or less legally. They can even set up their own firm if they wish, providing they have both the talent and capital necessary. Some government employees are now allowed to 'moonlight' and accept second jobs, and many more do so without permission. Part-time and casual work have proliferated during the 1990s. Local personnel exchanges have been established in major cities, allowing workers to register for transfers, which were once very hard to achieve. Wages, once stuck in a rigid 8-grade wage system, have also been freed up to some extent and become more flexible.

Despite such efforts, 'the iron rice bowl' often continues. This picturesque phrase means that one's job (which provides or fills the rice bowl) is totally secure (a rice bowl breaks if dropped, but an iron one does not). As a result, many employed people in China do not work hard and overstaffing is so common that people often sit reading newspapers or gossiping in the absence of any real work to do. Work incentives in state-run industrial or commercial firms, as well as the bureaucracy, are often few or totally absent. It is the private and joint venture firms that are making the running in improving worker efficiency. China is still a long way from having a true and efficient labour market.

In the consumer market many prices have been freed from the straightjacket of administrative price fixing and perhaps 90–95 per cent of prices now reflect supply and demand. Every effort to free prices for a group of items has meant an immediate price rise, because for decades prices were held artificially low. Increasing prices hurt urban dwellers in particular and the government tries to cushion the effect by providing a subsidy. This is too small to offset the price rise totally, but from the recipient's viewpoint it is better than nothing. It does, however, add to the recent intractable problem for the central government budget of having huge subsidies on the expenditure side, while revenues languish.

The currency of China, the *yuan,* is not fully convertible, although China has stated that it will move to this within five years as part of its intention to rejoin GATT. Along these lines, on 1 January 1994, China discarded the fixed exchange rate system and abandoned Foreign Exchange Certificates (FECs). These had discriminated against foreigners in China, who were forced to buy FECs at a very poor rate of exchange. The several exchange rates which existed are now unified and the *yuan* will be allowed to float, although this will be a 'dirty' or managed float, rather than a clean one. China hopes to use monetary and interest rate policies in order to stabilize the *yuan,* despite the fairly rudimentary nature of such economic tools in China. It is too soon to be sure, but China could eventually run into trouble here. If so, the authorities might be forced to step in and resume administrative controls which would involve backtracking for a while on the movement towards full convertibility.

Foreign investment is strongly sought by China which, after a slow and shaky start in the early 1980s, has managed to obtain a considerable amount. Despite economic fluctuations, caused by both domestic and foreign events, the flow of foreign investment has sharply increased. Between 1979 and mid-1993, total foreign funds invested in China amounted to some US$44 billion; official figures reveal that in 1992 alone they amounted to some $11 billion, while contracts were signed in that year for $57 billion worth. It is believed that four-fifths of total foreign investment comes from Overseas Chinese, often on the basis of Provincial ties and family relationships. Over half of the foreign investment comes from Hong Kong and Macao alone. Overseas Chinese investment tends to scatter more widely than non-Chinese foreign investment which restricts itself more to SEZs and the open cities.

China recognizes the importance of foreign investment and in 1992 some 97 per cent of all exports came from firms that had taken some foreign funding. The immediate policy on foreign investment (in 1994) is to try to focus it more in the areas of basic infrastructure and high technology. Only gradually will it be encouraged to expand further in the service areas.

Five Special Economic Zones have been established which offer concessions and draw many necessary services together in one area. In 1992 the SEZs were responsible for supplying 30 per cent of all China's exports. In addition to the SEZs, fourteen coastal cities have been opened to foreign investment and a myriad of tiny development zones have been established with relaxed rules but often with no location advantages, scattered over much of coastal China and even in parts of the underdeveloped interior. Many of these were ordered to be closed in 1993 to reimpose some central control and prevent competitive wastes. The provincial capitals of all coastal provinces are now accepting, and in almost all cases strongly seeking, foreign investment.

Since 1990, China has begun to move towards establishing free ports. Thirteen free trade zones have been set up around coastal harbours as a first step towards establishing free ports proper. At present they are in embryo stage and look very similar to SEZs. Foreign currency circulates within the free trade zones, while bonded warehouses help to reduce the number of bureaucratic restrictions and the time required to obtain needed imports.

The result of the new policies since 1978 mean that China is undergoing a major economic change which amounts to a small revolution. The economic reforms have begun to introduce market elements into what was a planned economy with a resulting mixture of State-run and private firms in both production and distribution. The process has been accompanied by confusion between the two systems and many leakages occur across the boundaries. Control by the planners has been drastically reduced, corruption flourishes and grows, but on the plus side much dynamism has been injected into the economy.

The overall economy has done well under the reform programme. So far, China has proved immune to the world recessions of the 1980s and early 1990s. Economic growth continues to be rapid in China, which has become one of the fastest growing economies in the world. So much so that the long-term government target of an average growth rate of 6 per cent until the year 2000 was increased to 8–9 per cent for the rest of the 1990s. The only problem that China faces in the area of growth is trying to slow it down. It proves difficult to moderate the ultra-rapid (around 10–15 per cent) rates without causing a major slump. The tools of fiscal and monetary policy, once non-existent, are still primitive and blunt. Despite some improvement, there are insufficient people with the skills or experience to implement fiscal and monetary policies properly. The process of slowing economic growth in China rather tends to resemble slowing a motor car down by running it into a brick wall. As such, the economic norm consists of a series of stop–go cyclical policies within a regime of high growth.

The happy problem of having undesirable high rates of economic growth regrettably brings inflation in its train. As a result, China's leaders regularly wish to restrain growth in order to contain this inflation. Although the data are of poor quality and often conceal the true level of inflation, when growth gets out of hand it can rise above 20 per cent in the cities. The Tiananmen incident, when the army put down students and workers who among other things were protesting against inflation, underlined the destabilizing dangers it can carry. Inflation is often feared among the older people, including China's leaders, as they experienced the great inflation of 1937–49 which helped to destroy the previous KMT government.

Inflationary pressures are endemic, partly but not entirely the result of rapid growth. Other reasons include the inability of the centre to raise enough revenue to cover expenditures; money supply blow-outs; slack credit control by banks especially at the provincial levels (where local officials often order the banks to lend to local schemes); local government investment sprees; expanding use of trade credit among the rapidly increasing number of firms; and speculative property booms.

The balance of payments suffers when growth is rapid and inflation worsens. The balance of trade tends to see-saw between surplus and deficit quite regularly. The deficits are partly the result of real economic growth sucking in imports and partly because the price rises make exporting more difficult as imports become cheaper. Quota and licensing controls over imports have steadily been reduced, but have not yet been eliminated. The ability to apply administrative import controls exists and these can be imposed without warning if the balance of trade deteriorates too much. When such controls are applied they tend to be relaxed as soon as the economic situation improves.

Foreign trade has expanded sharply as a result of the reform programme and China's movement back into the world. Foreign trade as a proportion of national income rose from 10.3 per cent in 1977, the eve of reform, to 36.9 per cent in 1991. China has promoted trade strongly and offers a good market for many products. The efforts of the many foreign investors in China have also boosted both exports and imports.

The southern province of Guangdong is an area of particularly high growth, especially around the Shenzhen SEZ and the Pearl River delta, including Guangzhou (Canton City). When the British colony of Hong Kong returns to China in 1997 it will add considerable economic muscle and weight to Southern China. Other major Chinese cities try hard to offer special concessions to foreign investment. Notable among them are Shanghai, Dalian and Tianjin, but many smaller cities are prepared to deal and offer concessions. The central government occasionally clamps down on those projects. This is usually because either a locally designated development area, or other special economic area, seems unlikely to succeed, or else some city or province is felt to be offering ludicrously large concessions. The situation is subject to change, but the overall policy has been to keep increasing the number of areas open to foreign investment and make the rules easier for foreigners.

Unemployment, previously concealed but considerable, has apparently reduced as a result of economic reform and higher growth rates. The real microeconomic reforms, which if implemented would reduce staff levels dramatically and release many people, have not been put into effect. Despite official statistics which suggest otherwise, the real level of unemployment is apparently still high. Underemployment is also a major problem, with much overstaffing in all state-run firms and organizations. Although the labour force is large, skills are often deficient at the local level.

Along with the adoption of freer market policies and the wide relaxation involved, the amount of central control has sharply diminished. The provincial and large city governments have gained more power. This reduction in central power causes consternation to some in Beijing. In practical terms, it has meant a fall in tax revenues which are gathered at local levels but are often not fully handed over to the centre. The taxation system is being reformed, but essentially involves farming out power: provincial governments negotiate how much they will hand over to the centre each year and then keep any surplus that they can raise. This favours the rich coastal and southern provinces. Naturally the provincial level governments try to keep as much for themselves as possible. There is no possibility of the central government replacing this lost tax revenue by profits from its own direct-run industry. First, many state-run firms have been privatized, while new ones are not being created. Second, previous tax reforms have increased taxation and reduced what is left as profit. Finally, about one-third of state firms lose money and admit it, while another third probably do so but manage to conceal it, so the profits are simply not there to be taken. The loss-makers survive only because the banks are instructed to keep extending loans to them, which of course adds to inflationary pressures by increasing the money supply.

The social scene

China had a large population for hundreds of years before it became a problem elsewhere in the world. Because of the large concentration of people in cities, effective social control mechanisms were developed.

These included the family being held responsible for the actions of any of its individual members and a really serious crime could lead to a whole family being executed. There was also a crude neighbourhood watch system where one family was responsible for reporting any antisocial behaviour by ten other families. People learned to get along with each other as there was no real alternative. The social system, with its emphasis on family, has altered in detail but has proved long-lived in approach, backed as it is by Confucian values. The rule of law, with its emphasis on responsibility for individual actions, has never been a feature in China.

Social policies since 1978, rather than taking centre place in their own right, have mainly tended to be spin-offs from economic and political changes. The social policies have included the following:

1   To encourage people to become rich; this compares with the past when this was actively discouraged.
2   To release latent entrepreneurial effort in order to kick-start the moribund economy and modernize quickly. It is very similar in essence to one of the goals of Thatcherism in Britain in the 1980s. Some of the results, such as a widening of income distribution, are similar too.
3   To try to contain corruption and reduce it, or at the very least prevent it from continually increasing.
4   To tackle crime in general and reduce its level. The crime rate has worsened, but it appears to be worse than it really is, because it is more freely reported than in the past. China still remains one of the safest places in the world to visit or live.
5   To try to slow the rate of growth of population and aim for a long term fall in the population. 'The one-child family' policy has been implemented widely, but with different degrees of severity depending on locality. Exceptions have been made for a few groups, such as minority peoples and for some who have a girl-baby the first time. Forced abortions, even late term, are common in those areas which impose the strictest control, but are unknown in slacker areas. By 1993 the family planning programme was showing signs of failure and a baby boom was underway. Chinese statisticians pointed out that the targets for future population sizes would not be met. The key reasons are rapid economic growth and reduced control; these are expected to continue, which casts pessimism over the likely success of family planning policy. This is the only social policy that was adopted in its own right, rather than being a spin-off from economic policy.

6   To allow private schools and education to cater for the needs and aspirations of the newly rich families. The state educational sector is under heavy pressure: teachers are poorly paid and inadequate in quality and many have left to earn more money elsewhere. The education sector is similar to virtually all of China's economic infrastructure, in that it is out of date and inadequate, while coming under heavy pressure from rapid economic growth. A new educational programme announced in 1993 hopes to revitalize the system, raise teachers' conditions by gradually increasing salaries and improve the quality and relevance of subjects taught. This will be financed in part by a special tax on businesses. It also foreshadowed the introduction of student tuition fees in higher education and a loan scheme for students from poorer families. Universities and other higher-level institutions will be allowed more power to manage their own affairs.

China is undergoing rapid social change and has been doing so since the 1980s. Some of the results have clearly emerged, others have not yet been noticed. China, an inward looking country over its entire history, tends to the secretive. Many quite ordinary events and statistics are regarded as not being a matter for foreigners and are deliberately hidden from outside view.

It is certain that since 1978 freedom is greater, incomes have increased and employment in agriculture has grown more slowly than in other areas such as industry, commerce, transport and production. Workers in private industry, including the self-employed, are now numerous and are better regarded in society. Until quite recently, a self-employed person was regarded as a failure, i.e. someone unable to get a proper job; now even university graduates sometimes opt to work for themselves rather than to join a state firm. A job in a foreign firm or joint venture is considered to be very desirable as it means earning more money and enjoying higher social status.

The increased freedom is genuine but has occurred within defined limits, although what these are at any particular time is often unclear. In addition, the lines keep getting redrawn. It is still not permissible to oppose the Party politically, support the Kuomintang in Taiwan, or ask for Western-style democracy. People are, however, freer to move. This was forbidden until recently, unless one was transferred (often forcibly) by one's work unit. People are often allowed to find jobs where they can, and although many move illegally, they do not seem to be punished much.

Private entrepreneurs have emerged and some are doing very well and are already in the millionaire league, even in terms of US dollars.

The majority of the Chinese are unarguably materially better off than they were a decade ago, some of them considerably so. The ability of some to pull well ahead of others causes resentment amongst those not able to increase their earnings sharply, as they feel as if they are being left behind.

Private workers and traders are allowed, partly because it is in line with general government policy, but also because of population growth and agricultural employment. Peasants are already too numerous for the needs of agriculture. The labour-intensive Maoist approach to agriculture was defended by some clever, if misled, Western sympathetic observers on the grounds that it was economically, socially and politically desirable. In fact, under that system peasants were born poor and stayed poor all their lives, while the growth in their numbers rendered improvements in agricultural techniques impossible. With the new economic policies people had to be encouraged to move out of agriculture and into other work. As they did so, the rate of growth of agricultural output roughly doubled, reflecting the existing low marginal productivity of labour and the newly released enthusiasm. Most of China's peasants are better off but still poor and a tiny proportion has become seriously rich.

The standard of living of the Chinese people has improved immensely as a result of the reform policies. The measurement of 'well-off-ness' using the traditional national income per head is misleading when applied to China and it severely underestimates the ability of people to buy things. Estimates by the IMF in the early 1990s, using 'purchasing power parity', indicate that rather than income being around the US$370 per head level as previously believed, it is actually closer to $1,600. This explains in part the intense interest by foreign businesses and governments in the China market and the ability of foreign firms to sell quite well there. China denies these figures and has a vested interest in trying to look poorer, as this gains it foreign market access, increases the ability to raise soft loans and may help to attract foreign investment.

The increased incomes both in and outside agriculture have led to changes in the patterns of consumption. In rural areas, the peasants have spent much on building new houses. There is a tendency to invest shrewdly much of their economic gains and if a family moves into its new house, the old one may be used for animal shelter. Local governments have also gone on construction spending sprees, sometimes for new buildings, often for roads, and occasionally for economic development zones.

In urban China washing machines were effectively unknown before 1980, but now many urban households have them. Other popular consumer items include colour TVs, hi-fis and personal computers. Newly married couples have a highly desired set of 'four items'. These now consist of refrigerators, TV sets, washing machines and video players. A few short years ago it was a more basic list consisting of watches, bicycles, sewing machines and clothing. Urban single children, who are widely regarded in China as rather spoilt and often referred to as 'Little Emperors', tend to have such items as electric toys and computer games lavished upon them.

The Chinese have traditionally eaten a lot of vegetables, but mostly from the necessity of poverty rather than choice. With the rise in income, chicken and pork have become reasonably common in the diet, as have eggs and even milk. Until recently, milk was restricted to invalids and the families of high Party officials. Western fast food has made an appearance in the cities in the past few years and despite being very expensive by local standards has been remarkably successful. Domestic tourism is on the increase and even visits to foreign countries are now possible. In short, China is in the process of doing a lot of catching up with the consumer preferences and habits of the outside world from which it was deliberately excluded for several decades.

The rapid economic development has begun to put pressure on existing social values. Accompanying this, there has been a noticeable resurgence of traditional values. This apparent contradiction can be resolved. Between 1949 and 1978 there was a determined effort to establish Marxist–Leninist–Maoist socialist thought and values into China. The economic growth, as well as political pressure against the Maoist vision, has eroded communist values. In addition, the newly allowed freedoms have allowed more traditional values to re-emerge. This includes not only Confucian family-centred thinking, which the communists had never managed to eradicate, but also many feudal practices and superstitions.

The result for society appears to be a confusing mixture of increased traditional values for many, together with the emergence of a small but wealthy middle class with more modern and Western values. There is still a definite feeling for the group among ordinary people and the sense of community is still strong. People look out for each other's interests more than in many Western cities and there is still an informal social watching of both each other and foreigners. This is not entirely antagonistic and can work for the benefit of people and encourage social harmony.

Overall policy assessment

China has tended to adopt a sort of balancing act which involves an approach of 'two steps forward, one step back'. This involves pushing forward as long as things are going well, then retreating as and when problems start to build up. After a pause, the process is resumed. The actual moves are often rather experimental in the first case, with several different methods being tried out and then the best one selected for widespread adoption.

On the political front, the only serious question mark is the future after Deng Xiaoping dies. Now in his eighties and with failing health, he cannot presumably live much longer. The economic gains made over more than a decade strengthen the position of the current leadership and increase the probabilities that present policies will continue after Deng dies.

In a historical perspective, China is still seeking a solution to the questions first asked after the ignominious defeat at the hands of British in the 1839–42 and 1856–60 Opium Wars. These questions included what were the best ways of dealing with these technologically advanced, if barbaric, foreigners and how to modernize China without losing Chinese social and cultural ways. These are universally regarded in China as superior to Western values. Whether China will eventually find a solution, and what this might be, is not certain.

The biggest overall question still to be answered is whether or not it is possible to run a country successfully with a communist government and a capitalist economy. To many Westerners it seems an obvious contradiction and a situation that must fail. This school of thought sees successful economic growth as inevitably increasing the pressure on a dictatorial regime until ultimately personal freedom must increase and the end result must be something approaching a Western democratic system. Such observers usually feel that the main historical question about what sort of China will be chosen is now in the process of being answered: a Western-style democracy, which will appear quite soon now.

This view may reflect Western cultural and political bias and some observers, although probably a minority, suspect that the end result in China, and perhaps other Asian nations, might not be a Western democracy at all. Instead, they might favour a sort of benevolent Confucian system, in which there is no real place for an opposition party, except perhaps a powerless nominal one as a sop to the disaffected and the intellectuals. Since it cut off from Malaysia in 1965, Singapore under Lee Kuan Yew has run a system that loosely fits this pattern, although to what extent this merely reflects the undoubted abilities and preferences of Mr Lee himself is uncertain. Western one-person-one-vote democracy, with its attendant lobbyists and pressure groups, which work for the benefit of the existing privileged and well-off, seems undesirable to many Asians. It is perceived as a weak form of government, which allowes undesirable social habits (drugs, prosti-tution, crime, homelessness etc.) to exist and even expand, despite the great wealth of the society. A Western democracy often seems to offer less benefits than could a benevolent ruler, schooled in the traditional values. At least if he makes a mistake he can, and will, reverse those policies which are damaging the nation. Democracies can struggle for decades to close down loss-making, heavily subsidized, industries and often cannot manage to achieve such closure. The result for the country is slower modernization and economic growth, as the system atrophies. Asian countries may not be prepared to take the risk of Western democracy, at least not for some considerable time.

Physical aspects and climate

Measured by area, China moved up to become the second largest country in the world, after Canada, when the USSR split into its component parts in late 1991. With a population at what seems to many Westerners an almost astronomic number of almost 1200 million at mid-1994, one person in every five in the world is both Chinese and living in China. Despite being a huge country, most of China consists of inhospitable mountains and deserts, much of it uninhabitable; only about 15 per cent can be used for arable farming and the worst 60 per cent cannot even be used for grazing animals. The majority of the people now live around the coast and up the river valleys and this situation will continue.

There are fifty-five minority peoples in China (excluding the major-ity Han) and they make up about 8 per cent of the population. There has long been a policy of sending Han Chinese to settle the inland areas, especially around the borders and wherever there is a local concentra-tion of minority peoples, who cannot be trusted in Chinese eyes. Tibet is a well-known example, but Xinjiang is another. Local people resent the Han Chinese, with their different language, culture and what is in effect nationality, but can usually do little effective about it.

Under the rule of Mao Zedong, there was a major effort to develop the interior and establish more regional development, moving atten-tion away from the coastal provinces. This was based on an idea of equity and what was proper. Sometimes the effort made some economic sense, but often it was a waste of resources, which were deliberately diverted from where they would have done more economic good to areas of greater need. This reduced the overall rate of economic growth and the long-term ability to help people, but satisfied a political desire to increase short-term equity. One reason that the coastal provinces are doing so well since the economic relaxation of 1978 is that they simply deserve to do so; they are the natural growth areas of China, and they had been starved of investment for decades. Putting in the investment allowed the coast to advance rapidly to where it should already have been.

As a huge country which approaches continental size, there is a range of climates and conditions, from bitter Siberian steppe weather in the north down to sub-tropical agriculture in the south. The best times to visit China, when you are less likely to suffer from either freezing cold or boiling heat, are autumn and spring. Most of China is then at a reasonable temperature and the damper southern areas are not too wet. This is of course the time of the year when hotels are likely to be fully booked and charging the highest rates.

China enjoys a winter monsoon, when icy cold air sweeps out of East Europe and Central Asia and has an effect all the way down to Hong Kong. The major cities for doing business in the northern parts include Beijing, Tianjin, Harbin, Shenyang and Jilin, and more minor include Xian and Zhengzhou. These are best visited in either autumn or spring. In winter, they are all bitterly cold, and it is unlikely that the temperature will rise more than a few degrees above freezing from mid-December to early March, although the actual starting and finishing time varies from year to year. The capital Beijing is often between −10 degrees and +4°C in that period, but the more northerly Manchurian area can get down to −40°C. The wind-chill factor can make it seem even colder than that. It is also a very dry climate and visitors often find that their lips get sore and crack easily. Around Beijing, in the late winter and spring, dust storms are common and unpleasant as the wind picks up sand from the desert. Many people wear face masks to avoid breathing in the dust, although some of the mask-wearers you see may simply have a cold or are hoping to avoid contracting one. The southern areas of China are very pleasant in winter, when the normal unpleasantly sticky weather disappears for a time. It can still get surprisingly cold, with overcoats needed even in southern Guangzhou, where it can on rare occasions even snow.

China also has a summer monsoon of the traditional type. This sweeps hot humid air up the coastal provinces and it can penetrate a good distance inland. In summer, the North is hot and dry, and the temperature may reach 40°C. The south is generally hot, sticky and unpleasant, and those unused to it may find it exhausting. Temperatures of 38°C with high humidity take their toll. It rains steadily in many southern areas and along the south-east coast typhoons can be a problem. Flights sometimes get cancelled if it rains and often cease entirely when a typhoon is approaching. As a consequence of having a continental climate the hottest part of China is not as might be expected in the deep south, but about half way up, inland from Shanghai. Wuhan, in the middle Yangtze River region, has a summer temperature higher than Guangdong in the south.

Part One
Appropriate Behaviour or
What to Do

1 *General points on proper behaviour*

1 Do note that China retains many Confucian values. Under the Confucian system the emphasis was on the need for properly ordered social relationships, in what was viewed as a sort of pyramid of roles. Rules and behavioural norms were generally accepted about how people were supposed to behave in relation to others. The belief was that if everyone could be educated to play their part properly, then society would be well run and general harmony would prevail.

More specifically, under the Confucian system, the family played a central role. The family head was responsible for the behaviour of the entire family and each person within the family had a clearly defined relationship to the others. A person's identity was established in part by the role played within the group. Members were referred to or addressed as 'elder daughter', 'younger brother', etc., reinforcing this role position. A crime by a family member could bring punishment on the whole family, including death for all, so the family controlled its individual members closely. Anyone without a family was generally pitied and regarded cautiously, even by the state.

There are several values that stand out in the Confucian system and many are still strong, although some have weakened as a result of the communist experience and the modernization now occurring. These are:

- 'Respect superiors', which applied both within the family and outside it. Outside the family circle, one's superiors in a firm had automatic respect by virtue of their position. Lower classes respected those above them. Listing from the top down, the class groups were scholars, officials, farmers, artisans and merchants. Scholars and officials made up 'the gentry' and at the very bottom were outcast groups such as actors, prostitutes, boat people and slaves. Within the family, 'filial piety' was the equivalent of respecting outside superiors. Not only was the family head to be obeyed, but elder brothers revered by younger ones, elder sisters by younger and so on. They commanded both respect and obedience. The widespread Chinese respect for age and seniority comes from such values; an older person is seen as more experienced, wiser and generally superior. People were educated and trained to know their place and to be content with it; deviations and rebellious behaviour were not tolerated. One practical consequence is that it may be hard to get a personal opinion in China, and the view or process set by higher authority will be followed and presented as not only correct but the views of the speakers themselves.

- 'Memorize lessons' was an important value in education. This still prevails in Overseas Chinese families, as well as in China itself. A common criticism of the students produced by the education system is that they merely learn by heart, to the detriment of understanding and being able to apply the lesson studied.
- 'Practise skills' was another rule and this is still current – indeed some believe that it is even more strictly observed these days than it was in older times.

2   Do remember that China is in a state of transition and rapid change. The traditional culture has been under pressure since about 1840 from contact with the West, economic development, civil war, invasion, decades of Marxist education, and now Western-oriented market policies. Recent pressures include a growing awareness of the outside world and its values, as the Chinese meet and talk to foreigners, see foreign films/TV/videos and exchange views with those who have returned from travelling or studying abroad.

Many traditional ways persist but change is underway, especially among the young and the city dwellers, but in contrast, some traditional values have reappeared after decades of being attacked or banned. Some people you deal with might be more traditional, while others may conform to more modern standards. Some might even be died-in-the-wool Marxists, although even here there are differences in beliefs and values. Some others will be very modern and be recognizably Western management types. This large range renders the identification and following of 'correct' behaviour more difficult.

The Chinese habit of fielding a large team where you are unlikely to know what each member is responsible for, or even to which organization he or she reports, can be a particular problem. There may not be one 'correct' attitude that will impress all members of their diverse team. When you add the fact that policy can change overnight and what was the proper policy or attitude yesterday is no longer valid today, you may not always find correct behaviour easy. Being aware of this is, however, valuable and can save you much frustration and worry.

Further, some Chinese who are actually still quite traditional have adopted modern 'foreign' ways when dealing with Westerners (e.g. using one hand, not two, to pass things to another person), but remain traditional when dealing among themselves. They will still observe and appreciate your sensitivity if you follow a traditional practice.

Still very strong values are attached to the Chinese family; group loyalty; the respect for hierarchy; and the preference for harmony. The traditional bureaucratic ways continue; personal ties and obligations are still stressed; and manual workers are often held in low esteem, although not as much as peasants, despite the propaganda. The values have weakened but are still present for female subjugation; kinship commitment (people sharing the same surname); and provincial allegiances. The traditional low esteem for soldiers has been raised by constant propaganda.

3   Facilities in China have improved immensely since the mid-1980s and continue to do so. Hotels are more comfortable, telephones work better and direct dialling is now a possibility, some nightlife has developed, including Western-style discotheques and Karaoke bars. Previously rarely available commodities, like instant coffee, or tonic to go with gin, are now commonplace; generally the variety and quality of consumer goods have improved remarkably.

4   The rapidity of change has caused high stress levels and changes can be abrupt. Since 1949 there have been many brutal campaigns and major social upheavals which increased tension at the time. A few short years after Chairman Mao died (1976), China altered substantially. The existing relatively orthodox Marxist economic system, which involved total job security, few price changes and an unchanging somewhat grey existence, was abandoned and new policies favouring market mechanisms were adopted.

The speed and degree of the changes have increased the level of stress. In Communist China, changes have always come abruptly and usually in unpredictable fashion. What was correct one day could be totally wrong the next; even the new situation could be reversed again if changes occurred in the high-level power structure. This is still the case, although the reformist group has dug itself in deeply.

5   Do be aware that the government is autocratic and unpredictable and, although generally benign, it can be ruthless if it feels the Party's or China's interests are seriously threatened. The Tiananmen massacre of June 1989 is an example of the extent to which the government will go if pressed. The Party controls the government and is itself split into factions, loosely a reformist pro-market moderate one led by Deng Xiaoping (which is in power), that is opposed by both an old-fashioned Stalinist central planning group and a small rump of extreme Maoist leftists.

6   Do note that the Chinese are intensely patriotic. There is a deep and unquestioned belief in China's historical, and cultural greatness. The Chinese name for China, 'Middle Kingdom', indicates that the world revolves around China at its centre. All Chinese are proud of their nation-race, and regard others as unfortunates, if not barbarians. Minority peoples within China are looked down upon and not really accepted as proper Chinese.

7   Do understand that Chinese are family and group oriented rather than individualistic. The family has long been the basic building block of the state and the centre of an individual's attention (see Note 1 above). Major personal decisions that in the West would be made by an individual were, and often still are, made on a family basis. Adding to this is the experience of communism, where group discussions were enforced and individuals who stood out could be punished later. At that time caution was so desirable that it could literally save one's life. The family-group model and communist experience means that many adult Chinese are reluctant to take decisions on their own. The group is a source of strength and comfort, and decisions are generally made on a consensus basis. A seemingly one-person problem in a factory may be solved by a decision taken only after extended discussion by the group. If you find that an individual Chinese person's attitude to a topic seems vague, it is often the result of the person knowing that the final decision must be by a group, not by one person, and he or she must be in line with that decision. The work unit commands a strong loyalty, not only because of the job-for-life approach adopted by the communist government, which is still the norm for many, despite recent

efforts to end it. The deferential attitude towards authority, the antagonism towards individualism, the persistence of a sturdy hierarchical structure (see Note 11 below) and lack of tolerance for deviance are all related to Confucian family values.

The importance of belonging to and identifying with a group spills over into the areas of humour and criticism. The Chinese do not tolerate irreverence (criticism of group or its leaders) or laughter at national or local leaders, policies or laws. The same applies to job allocation. For decades personal preferences counted for little and the need of the country (group) overrode these, so that people were simply told what they would study, what job they would do or where they would be sent. Decisions within the family on what career a child should try to pursue also tend to put family needs ahead of personal preference. Note that, unlike the Japanese, the Chinese never bow, but frequently you will shake hands with every single member of the group.

8 Do note that your group needs a strong, identifiable leader. The leader was probably decided before you left your country, but if not you must choose a leader who will play a strong role. On all documents that go to the Chinese and include a list of members, do put the leader's name first. Tell the Chinese who the leader is, and he introduces people and speaks first, he gets the best seat, etc. A woman leader is acceptable, as you are foreign, but it is uncommon for the Chinese to have one. You will find that the Chinese tend not to like a foreign group splitting up to do different things, as they feel that the group is a team and should behave like one. A group is assumed to have a common purpose, with a leader who makes decisions for all. It is best to do all your arguing in private and present a united front in public. If the Chinese hear different opinions expressed within a group, for instance about what members would like to see or do, it confuses and upsets them.

9 Do understand that the Chinese view people as essentially either 'insiders', who belong to the group or unit, or 'outsiders', who are strangers. The latter can be treated with an indifference that can border on contempt. Trying to get assistance from another organization can be trying, as the people there feel no responsibility to assist, indeed quite often they feel the reverse. In order to secure cooperation between organizations it is usually necessary to have a higher official intervene and order compliance. Where help from another unit is obtained, this unit will often be rather antagonistic and may try to gouge with a high price or take other uncooperative action. Other than the family, network groups to which a Chinese might belong include the work unit, school or university class peers, people from the same province, or members of the same military service unit or delegation a person might have been on.

10   Note that with regard to letters, the Chinese often feel no obligation to reply if it is from someone unknown; the sender is an outsider. This lack of response does not have the feeling of rudeness that would accompany such action in the West. You should be aware, however, that a lack of reply often means 'no'.

11   Do remember China is a hierarchical society and rank counts for much. This is, of course, part of the traditional Confucian values discussed above (see Note 1 above). Everyone is slotted into a complex system of superior and subordinate. A person's place is not fixed and he or she can rise or fall within the ranks, but the ranks themselves continue unchanged. Within the family a person's place is fixed, so that the elder sister is always the elder sister and treated accordingly, but in business people may rise and fall and their treatment changes accordingly. This can cause resentment and hurt feelings, so that office politics loom large in China, and most enterprises contain various factions. Because everyone lives within a rigid hierarchy, and harmony must prevail, specific rules of social conduct are laid down, and are strictly taught to all children.

Bureaucracy is an ancient Chinese art form and the bureaucracy, like society, is strictly hierarchical in rank. The privileges of every level, and person, are clearly defined or recognized. Foreign visitors and residents are approached in the same vein. The level of a visitor is determined by the Chinese and the higher in status is your firm's representative, the higher up the ladder of seeing officials he or she can get. You should send someone with the highest credentials possible, as the higher your rating, the more that will be done for you. Expertise is, of course, also necessary.

Former heads of state etc. are usually well respected and treated because of their previous position, irrespective of their current status or past behaviour and record. Members of a foreign aristocracy are also revered and, interestingly, this was true even in the extreme days of the Maoist period.

12   The Chinese tend to go for the best and for the most prestigious product or technology. This is partly the result of the Confucian heritage, the value system and their hierarchical view of the world. It is also much safer for a Chinese to buy the best, for a superior is less likely to criticize him for this. The Chinese also like to deal with the 'best' firm and gain kudos from this, because of lingering fears that they may be cheated by foreigners. Officials also tend to choose the best in order to avoid any possible criticism. It is not unlike many purchasing officers in Western firms in the 1980s, who preferred to buy IBM personal computers at a high price rather than perfectly satisfactory and substantially cheaper clones.

The latest 'cutting-edge' technology is almost always preferred. Rarely will the most appropriate be chosen over the most prestigious, which means that sales pitches along the lines of being suitable for Chinese conditions may fall on deaf ears or even be seen as mildly insulting. The Chinese will compare your product or technology with what else is available internationally. Once used to the best, the Chinese are very brand-loyal, and do not seem to like having to make new decisions among the variety of choices offered by Western market systems. Although they make a big thing about 'old friends', they are willing to dump an old friend if a really superior product appears, particularly if it is internationally recognized as the best.

13 Observe that harmony is generally sought. This does not preclude the Chinese from suddenly becoming forthright and even turning downright rude in their dealings, but such a switch is almost always tactical and a part of a negotiating strategy (see Chapter 12, Note 24). Harmony is an important part of the Confucian heritage and is also sought in countries such as Japan, South Korea and Singapore. It is believed that if everyone in society plays their proper role, then overall harmony will be preserved. For this reason, self-discipline and moderation are essential components of human behaviour. For most foreigners, harmony is best preserved by avoiding confrontations, maintaining temper and smiling rather than looking angry. Trying not to cause anyone to lose face is also an important part of preserving harmony.

14 Good manners in China usually means being self-deprecating. If flattered, one must deny what was said. Saying 'thank you' when complimented in any way is quite wrong, and would appear extremely arrogant to the Chinese. Good responses include 'I do not deserve it', 'Oh no, no', 'You are much too kind', 'I am really only a beginner', 'I still have a lot to learn' and 'You are very polite but I must deny it'.

When trying to sell to the Chinese you face a problem in this respect. They wish to buy the very best (so you have to demonstrate that your product or technology is that) but you are not allowed to boast that it is the best! One way round this may be to produce a glowing review by some third party, if you are able to do this, or perhaps show sales figures and graphs that display very good growth rates, and then use deprecating words, like 'Some consider we are not too bad' or 'We find other firms often imitate our product'. The Chinese will then realize just how good is the product and its performance, but you have avoided unseemly boasting.

15   Do recognize that most Chinese are superstitious and even well-educated, apparently Westernized Chinese have many beliefs of a superstitious nature. Most, perhaps all, important decisions will be deferred until an optimal time. This will be determined by fortune-tellers or by reference to books that are readily available. Unexplained delays in negotiations may be due to such factors, as well as the better-known bureaucratic ones. Various superstitions exist, and they vary in different parts of China, so that it is not easy to know what a particular person will believe in. Homonyms abound in the Chinese language, which is essentially monosyllabic so that one sound may stand for many different things and even a simple beginner's dictionary will have perhaps 50 different meanings for the word 'li'. The number of homonyms means that some words are regarded as lucky or unlucky because they happen to sound like a completely different word with a good or bad meaning. Some, for example, believe that it is good to see a deer, as it has a homonym which means 'prosperous'.

Numbers have a special significance for the Chinese. Most Cantonese believe that the numbers 4, 44, 444 and so on are very bad as they are a homonym for death; they would not buy a motor car with such a licence plate or stay in a hotel room with such a number. Eight is, however, seen as good. Odd numbers were traditionally seen as masculine, even ones as feminine, and odd numbers were generally preferred. Three is a good number as is five, which is probably connected with an old belief in five elements, five grains and five tastes as well as the old imperial ranking system of officials. Seven is also often seen as a lucky number, as are multiples of it such as 14, 21 or 35. Nine was a very lucky number, and 81, the square of nine, particularly so, and you might notice that almost all ancient gates in China have 81 stud heads on them.

Colours play an important part in superstitions. White is the colour of death and should never be worn in an unrelieved form – a red tie with a white shirt or red buttons on a white dress would, however, render it very acceptable. Red is a particularly good or happy colour in much of Asia, including Japan and South Korea. In parts of China even white bread loaves have a splash of a red edible dye on them to make them look more attractive. Yellow can also be associated with death, although a darkish yellow was also linked with the emperors of history (only they could have yellow roofs on buildings) and with some monks. Blue and white together or blue and yellow together also suggested death.

Be aware that some believe that no important decisions at all should be taken in July for superstitious reasons. This means that it is not a good month to negotiate.

16 Do observe that Chinese tend to stand closer to you than you are probably accustomed to or like. Try not to let it grate on you and do try to avoid stepping backwards a small step – if you do this a Chinese will usually advance to fill the gap and then you are forced back again. The end result looks as if you are both engaged in a slow dance step together. If you are lucky, the person will not have been eating garlic or curry.

17 Note that eye contact is important but can mislead. Many Chinese become worried if they are talking and the listener, although concentrating, stares out of the window. Frequent eye contact when addressing someone is desirable. You should be aware, however, that traditionally it is bad manners to gaze into the eyes of a total stranger, so do not be alarmed if, on intro-duction, a person does not look straight at you. Guard against your instinct which might tell you that the person you are meeting is shifty and untrustworthy; it is merely different body language. Also note that the Chinese often do not smile when introduced, but this does not mean they are unfriendly, it is merely a different social custom. A smile is not always friendly, and it can indicate embarrassment, especially if it is rather fixed and occurs in response to a statement by you. A smile may conceal anger also, again usually in response to something said or done.

18 Do take warm clothing for winter wear and note that Chinese clothing sizes may be too small for you. In winter you should expect to be cold when outside, but note that it can also be bitterly cold inside some official offices and buildings. At the same time, you might well find it too hot in your hotel. With magnificent disregard for climate, on 15 April all furnaces for heating buildings are turned off until 15 November, when they come on again. In the far north it is extremely cold and you are ill advised to visit in winter. If you must go then, take 'long-johns' and warm underwear. Women as well as men in China typically wear long-johns under trousers as the country is poor and the heating in houses and workplaces is often inadequate or non-existent. You can actually be colder inside buildings in the middle of China than in the north, as regulations restrict the heating of buildings south of the Yangtze River.

If you try to buy clothes in China you will probably be disappointed; the quality is still not great (the best is exported), colours are limited, designs are basic and in many cases the sizes available are too small to fit average-sized Westerners. Buying a large enough pair of shoes can be difficult and if you have to buy some, start by asking if they have anything that would fit at all.

19   Do expect to meet a lot of cigarette smoking when in China. Cigarettes are cheap, but the brands are usually very strong, so that few Westerners really like them. Probably because Chairman Mao was a chain smoker, there was no publicity allowed in China about the ill effects of smoking during his lifetime. Few Chinese realize that these days smoking is offensive to many Westerners. Unless you cannot bear it, you are advised to ignore the smoke and try not to look concerned.

20   Do buy medicines in Hong Kong before entering China. Even if you are in good health you may well fall ill in China, especially with minor ailments like colds and upper respiratory tract infections. Take with you what you might need. When you have a cold, it is amazing how a lemon-flavoured aspirin hot drink in your hotel room can improve the way you feel. Pain killers, throat lozenges, antibiotics and anti-diarrhoea tablets are a must. You should also take a good portable short-wave radio with you to keep in touch with world events. China is simply different from other countries, it is easy to feel cut off and isolated, and many visitors suffer from a mild version of culture shock, especially if on their own. A radio-cassette player can make a lot of difference, especially if you take some of your favourite tapes with you.

21   Do expect a long lunch-hour rest period. In China, many people start work early in the morning and it is common to stop work for a very long lunch break of perhaps two or even two and a half hours. After eating lunch, many Chinese take a siesta, then wake up refreshed for the afternoon work. As noon approaches, if you find you are being hurried back to the hotel, or the meeting you are in is showing signs of being halted, this is probably the reason. Despite improvements, it can still be difficult to make telephone calls in China, but note that it is particularly difficult to reach anyone between noon and about 2.30 pm. As few foreigners take a siesta, it means that they often get tired visiting or working in China.

22   Most Chinese work a six-day week and you will be expected to do so too. Refusing to do this and demanding leisure might cause the Chinese to feel you are something of a dilettante and not a serious or proper person with whom to do business. They might, on the other hand, sometimes suggest you take off more time for leisure, usually if they are having trouble reaching agreement among themselves or gaining approval from higher up or from another unit.

23   Most Chinese have three names, with the surname coming first on their business card. A few Chinese have but two names, and a very few have as many as four. In all cases, the surname will come first on a card or list, so that Peng Lian is 'Mr Peng'. If he or she has a title such as Director of an Institute it is polite to address him or her by the title, and you should do so. You say 'Director Peng' or 'Vice-Chairman Wang' rather than plain Mr or Madame. 'Madame' is often used for officials rather than 'Mrs', as it sounds more imposing, and for years in Communist China, 'Mrs' had a rather derogatory feel of referring to a woman who was wealthy, but rather empty, selfish and uncaring.

24   Do note that travel and sightseeing are particularly tiring in China, as so much is different. The mind is continually being exposed to new sights, ideas and behaviour patterns, while you are cut off from what seems 'normal' to you. This is a mild form of culture shock, and can be surprisingly exhausting. It can also lead to bad temper and anger.

25   Do expect to wait around the hotel a lot or be sent on sightseeing trips. You may find you spend what seems to be an inordinate amount of time in such ways. This can be both boring and tiring. Sightseeing trips are often suggested, partly because the Chinese wish you to be happy and to understand something of their past. More practical reasons may include that some essential Chinese meeting has not yet occurred; someone has not yet

decided what should be done; or perhaps they have decided that you are impatient and are likely to make more concessions if they spin out things so that not much seems to be being achieved.

26 Do expect to feel you are a foreigner when in China and be aware of the ambivalent attitudes. The people and culture are quite different from most Western societies and you will feel different too. Many Chinese are ambivalent about foreigners. On the one hand, they admire and respect foreigners for their achievements and advanced technology which, they think, can improve China considerably; on the other, they feel that foreigners are inferior, lack culture and manners, and in some cases their nation may have treated China badly in the past. At the individual level, this can mean that some Chinese are fascinated by foreigners and others repelled. But all Chinese will see you as a foreigner and rather inferior in many respects. The things about foreigners that most upset many Chinese are greed and profit seeking, overly sharp business practices, rowdy unseemly behaviour, loud foreign pop music and anything connected with sex and drugs. Most Chinese feel that they can learn much from foreign technology but little or nothing from foreign social or philosophical teachings. Even the communism in China was very Chinese, and until Liberation in 1949, many top-ranking communist leaders knew surprisingly little of European Marxist thought. You will find that rural Chinese expect more Chinese-style manners and behaviour from you than the urban ones you will usually deal with, as the latter are both more tolerant and used to dealing with 'barbarians'.

27 Note that the Chinese have a view of other nationalities which is often based on an unpleasant historical relationship. The lessons and experience of history are more important to educated Chinese than they are to most foreigners. The Chinese are well versed in their own history and often refer to it for relevant examples and analogies for the present. They have also been well taught about the actions of a few foreign nations that have impinged strongly upon China, especially invasions, colonization of parts of China and unfair treaties forced upon the Chinese when a war was lost. Rather like the Irish, the Chinese are very history-aware and bitterness persists. As a result, the natural suspicion of foreigners, common, it seems, to all nations and races, is reinforced if you happen, for example, to be British or Japanese.

Americans are often seen as open, warm and trusting, but rather child-like and naive as a result. Considered to be essentially shallow with little history and culture to boast of, Americans are easily perceived as brash, arrogant and pushy, as well as impatient and lacking in proper self-discipline.

The Japanese tend to be seen as hard-working, efficient, successful and extremely loyal to their firm and to Japan. Japanese success at coping with Western impact during and after the nineteenth century is admired. On the negative side they are often seen as cruel (the legacy of occupation and Japanese behaviour during the 1930s and 1940s); too dominating and hegemonic; and essentially untrustworthy or two-faced. Japanese manners are seen as excessively polite and irritating and cause many Japanese individuals not to be trusted. The Japanese may be seen as self-serving and not interested in helping China, which many Chinese think they should, as Japan is seen as owing a debt to China, as well as being wealthy in its own right. The Japanese are also seen as being willing to take advantage of Chinese weakness or ignorance and not behaving as friends should. Privately, some Chinese still refer to Japanese as 'poisonous dwarves', a common term of political abuse during the Maoist era.

The South Koreans are seen as a stubborn people, and more hard-working than the Chinese. They are not particularly liked, but are often preferred to the Japanese. After all, China successfully invaded Korea on occasion, but Japan invaded China, a keenly felt insult and failure for the Chinese.

The British are reasonably well regarded, especially considering the rather sad history of colonial occupation of China. The English are seen as clever, quite sophisticated considering they are foreigners, but with an unfortunate tendency to be rather cold, holding themselves aloof, and never really becoming involved much. They are seen as often deliberately holding people at arms' length.

Australians are seen as acceptable, but rather brash, slightly abrasive and lacking in sophistication. They tend, however, to be trusted as the Chinese have discovered that they say what they think. As a consequence, a closer relationship can often be gained than, say, with the English, as long as the 'big' and boisterous Australian behaviour is contained or abandoned.

28 Do clap back if you are applauded. The Chinese show appreciation of a person or group by clapping hands, and you may be welcomed to an institute such as a school, or to a meeting, in this way. Chinese good manners dictate that you must clap back, although less vigorously and preferably with a small smile and nod of the head.

29   Do recall that China is a secretive society. The Chinese have long seen information about their country and society as a matter for themselves alone. You may come across the phrase 'This is not a matter for foreigners', which may be applied if you ask what a scuffle in the street is about, or if you see criminals being paraded around town on lorries. The tendency towards secrecy is such that even at universities one can find that economics books are only available to economics students, law books to law students, and so on. This is part of the insider–outsider distinction which permeates the Chinese way of thinking. Unlike in most developed countries, the Chinese are used to not getting information from their own government or other units, and are equally accustomed to not passing on information to others.

30   Do note that using the telephone may be difficult. It is not always easy to place a telephone call and get through. Direct dialling is now possible in some modern hotels. When the call goes through, however, you will often find that the person at the other end has a tendency to shout rather than speak normally, so that a truly private telephone call is not always possible. The person answering the telephone may be less than helpful and have an attitude resembling that of a gatekeeper. You may be interrogated as to why you wish to speak to a particular person and clearly there may be little intention of putting you through unless satisfactory answers are received. If you are able to leave a message, and many gatekeepers will simply refuse to take one, it might get to the right person but in too many cases it simply seems to languish around a desk or even be thrown out. You are a victim of being an 'outsider' trying to get inside, and the person answering the telephone may feel no obligation to help you in any way, including passing on the message. You might find yourself cut off in mid-call too, depending on the hotel and which part of China you are in. You are advised to fax if possible, as this method gets round the gatekeeper barrier mentality.

   If you think you might wish to make contact in the future with someone you meet, you should take down their telephone number, and, if they have one, their fax number. If you do not do this, you may find it next to impossible to work your way through the bureaucracy to locate them again. There is, in any case, a general attitude of secrecy about information, including telephone numbers, so that switchboards are often unhelpful when you are trying to find someone. You might also find the person answering merely says hello ('wei') and refuses to state the name of the organization even when you ask. The 'gatekeeper' might reluctantly reveal the firm's name if you ask (correctly) if it is the so-and-so company, but might not be willing to identify the unit otherwise. You should state the name of your company, rather than your personal name, as this often gets more respect, and be prepared to explain why you are calling, what the issue is, etc. rather than merely be put through. The word 'wei' is often repeated during calls, which is sometimes a way of ensuring you are still there, in view of the lost connections caused by poor equipment, or it may be simply to fill a gap in the conversation.

31   Do expect transport problems and bad traffic conditions. Most large Chinese cities have traffic problems, with Shanghai being the worst, but fortunately many people travel by bicycle. Although they may wobble about in the road or even fall off in front of your car, at least it means that motor vehicles are less held up than if everyone had a car. The reason that people fall off at low speeds is that only one size of bicycle is widely available and it is too large for many small-built Chinese and they cannot actually reach the road surface with their feet, even when sitting on the crossbar. Luckily, long experience has made people adept at balancing when virtually stationary, thus reducing accidents. If, however, one person should happen to fall off when balancing at almost zero speed at a red traffic light, this may knock over several others, on the domino principle. With the rapid economic growth in and after the later 1980s, commercial vehicular traffic has built up in most cities, while young males hurtling about on low-powered motor bicycles have become something of a hazard.

If travelling by bus, which is cheap but often extremely crowded, do expect a savage scramble to board; you should not hesitate to use your superior weight and height to avoid being left behind. Once on board, you may find that attitudes change; you are now a temporary 'insider' and part of the crowd. You may be embarrassed to be offered a seat by some little old man or woman who clearly needs it more than you. If no one offers you a seat, some activist type might start a small mass movement to bully someone to offer you one – which is even more embarrassing. It is easier to give in and take the seat, as the person who offered will lose face if you refuse it; if the offer of a seat came as a result of a public argument, a refusal by you would mean that more people would lose face.

Buying train tickets can be difficult as far more people wish to travel than there are seats available. You must book in advance, like everyone does, but you might find that no seats will be sold until three days before the date of travel, and the line of people waiting to book is several hours long. Many foreigners are walked to the front of the line by some official and forced to jump the queue. This may seem unjust and embarrass you, but it does save you many hours' queuing, and to refuse is difficult and would cause a severe loss of face to the official. Mostly whichever host unit is responsible for you will send someone to do all this for you, and you might be totally unaware of the difficulties.

You should also be aware that aircraft flights are often cancelled without warning. In some remoter parts of China, the aircraft may not fly if it starts to rain, although this problem seems to have reduced in the last few years. You might well find that a seat previously booked and confirmed is suddenly no longer available, so it is wise to keep checking you still have a seat. Chinese airlines have at last put in a computerized system but some booking is done by hand: if someone starts in the south to fly to somewhere in the north, the people mid-way may not know how many are already on-board and therefore overbook locally. You might be able to get on if you can produce documents from some important organization or person to show you must get there that day, etc. A rudimentary knowledge of Chinese helps here, especially if you can ingratiate yourself. Someone may well have just had you bumped off the flight because of 'pull', and you should not be ashamed to try to bump someone else off in turn.

32 Be prepared to be constantly asked standard questions, some rather personal. Common questions are, where are you from, how many times have you been to China, have you been to Beijing or their home city/province, can you speak any Chinese, and do you like Chinese food and can you get it in your country? Many questions might seem extremely personal and even impertinent to foreigners; for example, how old are you, have you been divorced, how much did your suit cost, or what salary do you earn? Chinese comments are often banal, such as 'yours is a big country', or 'you have come a long way', and it may leave you with little obvious to say. If they have asked if you are married and have children, you can return the question. If they have a son, remember to compliment them on this, as male children are preferred, but do not, of course, commiserate if they have a girl. The one-child policy of the government means that such people will probably never have a son and may resent it keenly.

33 Do remember which are safe and unsafe topics of conversation. As in most countries, safe topics include the weather, the country you are in and your own country. It is also fine to discuss language and the difficulties of learning both Chinese and your own language, as well as such things as the availability of reading materials. You might be gently asked if you could send them an English magazine to read – if so, agree and make a note of this at once. It might provide you with a favour that they will have to repay later. It is safe, indeed wise, to ask if they have travelled outside China and if they have been to your country. Other safe topics are Chinese history, art and culture; the importance of the family unit; the differences between China and the West (although you may find that the Chinese are not really interested in the West except to be polite), and the progress that China has made. Chinese medicine is also safe and an interesting topic.

Unsafe topics include all discussions of Chinese politics, leaders or government decisions. If you know the person well and are circumspect in approach, you could ask about their experiences in the Cultural Revolution, but this is best avoided otherwise. It is best to avoid discussion of international politics as you can inadvertently cause offence here and probably never know it. Do not criticize Chinese food, as this is a central part of the culture, and it is unwise to comment unfavourably, even as a joke, if you were offered something unpalatable or even offensive to you, like sea-slugs, snakes, pigeon heads or bears' paws. The topic of sex or anything connected with it like strip clubs should be avoided, as should the poor amenities and relative poverty of China. You should avoid criticizing anything at all, as it may cause them to pull away from you and destroy the harmony.

34 Do expect restaurants to close early. In Beijing they often open for evening meals around 4 pm and close by about 8.30 pm. The Chinese have the habit of eating early; if invited out, 6.30 pm is a likely time to meet at the restaurant. If in Beijing, it is worth asking if your embassy has a bar and a regular get-together time for visitors. It can provide a welcome rest from culture shock. The Australian Embassy used to have a very popular get-together for all foreigners early every Friday evening, from which people often went on to dinner at a hotel. It is worth checking to see if this is operating when you are in Beijing.

35   Do expect to be frustrated in China. Many things happen that are inexplicable and can annoy. Even more things do not happen that you think should. Delays are common and it is just about impossible to find out why you are being kept waiting for days on end, hanging around the hotel waiting to see someone, or perhaps for a decision to be made and passed down. The culture is quite different and some values or behavioural practices are not the same, which can be a source of frustration. The bureaucracy is huge and impenetrable, machinery and equipment are often ancient and work badly, and inefficiencies abound. Putting it all together, a frustrating experience is normal.

2 Approaching China

1 Do select a good Chinese name for yourself and product. Names
are very symbolic for the Chinese, and company names such as
'Happy something', 'Delightful something' or 'Prosperity
something' are quite common. You cannot change the name of
your foreign company to suit Chinese culture, but you can ensure
that the actual Chinese characters selected mean something nice
and attractive, rather than neutral or even actively repellent.
Imagine the amusement in your country if you found a foreign
company called 'Fly-by-Night Removals' or 'Sewage Ice Cream'
and you will appreciate how things can go wrong. Similarly, your
personal name should be attractive when put into Chinese
characters.

2 Do make the initial contact by mail. The China Council for
Promotion of International Trade (CCPIT) is a good starting
place and they can ensure that you get off on the right track.
The Chinese embassy in your country is another good place to
contact and you should ask them to introduce you to a suitable
foreign trade corporation or ministry in China. You should also
approach your embassy in Beijing as it has, or should have,
experience, contacts and *guanxi*. This means a special personal
relationship of some strength, and includes the idea of a debt
that has been incurred and that must be repaid. It lies at the heart
of many business and other dealings in China.

The proposal itself should include more than you would
normally send in the West. You might send a complete description of your firm, its history, its share of the market, a recent
profit and loss statement or annual report, the ownership profile
and director list, as well as a detailed description of the product
and a lot of technical information to show its quality and performance. It is better to send a mass of information on a few main
products you have to sell, rather than skimpy information on
many. If you send information about a lot of products and some

come under the auspices of different Chinese institutions, be it end-users or ministries, it will not be clear to a Chinese where exactly to send the information, so he or she might simply not do anything with it at all.

You are trying to convince the Chinese that you are worth dealing with and are not someone who will let them down or try to rob them. There is a deal of suspicion about Western firms in China which you have to overcome. Send references or a copy of a magazine or newspaper article about your firm if you are able. You should specify exactly what you wish to do, sell a good or technology, buy what kind of items, etc. and also the sort of business arrangement you are interested in discussing, as well as a suggestion as to where and when you might meet in China.

The letter must be translated into Chinese as well as being in English, but the rest of the material can be in English if you cannot get a translation done, although a translation is highly desirable. This must be in modern Chinese, using simplified characters, and avoiding archaic expressions or any vocabulary or expressions associated specifically with Taiwan or South-east Asia. It is far easier to jump the first hurdle and get someone interested in you and your product if the first people you approach can read about you immediately in their own language. It also shows that you are taking the proposal seriously and working hard at it. Do send several copies of your initial proposal package, a dozen is not too many, so that it can be considered quickly by several people and not be unnecessarily delayed. Copying machines are scarce in Chinese institutions.

You should try to put forward the highest credentials you can because the higher your rating, the more that will be done for you and the more important people you can see. They can then drop the word down the line to help you.

It is useful to ask for an acknowledgement of your letter whenever you write to someone, especially for the first time, as it is common for Chinese not to respond to letters (see Chapter 1, Note 10). If an agent or intermediary is drawn to your attention, write to him or her also. The use of intermediaries as opposed to a direct approach has a long history, and if you come recommended by someone known to a firm, you will be taken much more seriously. A letter out of the blue might be simply ignored.

3   Do use a liaison officer or help-mate resident in China, and preferably someone Chinese. This should be someone who knows the ropes and has many contacts in positions of authority. He or she can help you see the right people, choose the most appropriate firm to deal with, check up on the interpreter's ability, keep you informed about private discussions in Chinese within the opposite team and perhaps spot body-language signals that you would not understand. As a local resident, the liaison officer can also look out for your interests after you have left China. Before signing any document it is important to let the liaison officer read it over to see that it is satisfactory. There are firms that specialize in such work and for an up-to-date list, contact your embassy and CCPIT. It is important not to accept at face value any claims by a person to be a representative of the government, but check up on anyone who approaches you. They may simply be individuals with little to help you touting for business.

4   It is most important to have your business card in both English and Chinese, and it must contain all your titles within the company, and any awards you may have earned such as academic degrees or any honours you may have been given. Such items on the business card are found impressive. The cards can be printed in Hong Kong quickly and cheaply, but you should take an example or model with you, in modern simplified characters, which can simply be copied. In many Western countries you can now get such cards made but they will usually be more expensive. When exchanging cards, it is polite to hold your card in both hands as you present it. This is an old-fashioned courtesy which many Westernized Chinese no longer do with foreigners, but they will notice and appreciate it if you do. They may even remark that you are familiar with the traditional culture or something of that kind, and this can provide you with an opportunity to strengthen the personal relationship. It is useful to write your hotel name and room number on the card before you present it, so that the person can contact you. Prepare cards in advance, in your hotel room, and do not underestimate the number you will need. Each person in the Chinese team should get one of your cards. If you run out during the day, make sure the leader of the group gets a card, smile and apologize to the lower-ranking members, and make sure you stock up for the morrow.

Who to send

5   Do send as team leader an experienced, older person but with expertise and who is a friendly and sensitive type. If possible,

you should send an experienced, senior and older person as the team leader, because of the hierarchical nature of the society. It also shows that you are serious in intent and are committed to a long-term presence. Age is revered in China, and Confucius felt that a person was not mature until they reached 30 years of age. Age is part of the hierarchy of status in China and grey hair is a definite plus. An active 40-plus-year-old man who has a grey beard will be esteemed both for age (the Chinese will assume he is about 60 years old) and the energy he evinces. A business person needs experience so that obvious gaffes can be avoided. Previous experience with the Chinese in South-east Asia would be helpful.

You can safely send a woman as leader to China, as the Chinese regard your foreignness as much more significant than your gender. This contrasts with Japan and many Middle Eastern countries.

A team is necessary, because one person is not likely to be able to answer all the questions asked. Trying to economize by sending a sole person is usually a mistake, unless you are testing out the water and are not intending to negotiate at all on the first visit. In addition, in traditional China, the actual negotiation was the work of underlings, so that if you go alone you must do all the work and hence lose face. You will normally need an engineer/technician, a few sales representatives, and a high-level senior leader.

Those sent in the delegation should preferably be warm, friendly, flexible, tactful and sensitive types. This is, of course, desirable whatever foreign country you are visiting, but Asian societies, with their different social rules and sensitivity to what is not said, require particularly delicate treatment for success. Sincere friendliness is needed, and the Chinese are adept at recognizing fake emotions as they have a lifetime of experience of deciphering concealed ones. Flexible attitudes, patience, not losing one's temper or becoming irritated, and the energy to work long weeks while under stress are desirable. You might find yourself climbing hundreds of steps as you are sent on visits to temples, etc., while the Chinese are meeting to consider the proposal and you have nothing to do. It can be a tiring process. You are quite likely to go down with a cold or sore throat also, as you will have little resistance to the local bugs.

You should try to send someone who can either drink alcohol very well, which can be most useful at Chinese banquets when the toasting begins, or else a teetotaller. The latter is acceptable as a lot of Chinese do not drink and many turn bright red with even a small amount of alcohol inside them, which embarrasses them so they prefer to avoid it. The Chinese understand if you plead an allergy.

If selling, as part of the team you will need a well-qualified technician, familiar with the nuts and bolts, as questions will be asked that require detailed familiarity with the product or technology, from the very start of manufacture to its capabilities in final use. Bringing your own interpreter should be regarded as essential (see Chapter 3, Note 24).

6 It is often desirable to have an Overseas Chinese as part of your team, as they will be much more culturally aware, help to avoid mistakes for your side, and (if not solely Cantonese or other dialect speakers) can understand what is being said. It is vital that you do not rely upon them to translate, as translators are not regarded as a part of the team by the Chinese, and it will reduce the status of the Overseas Chinese member sharply. Both they and the local Chinese will be aware of this. A major advantage of having an Overseas Chinese on the team is that outside the meetings the Chinese will often approach him or her and explain what they really wanted or meant earlier in the meeting, or sound him or her out about issues and 'fly kites' about new proposals. This can be extremely useful in negotiations. They do this as part of the preferred indirect approach and seeking harmony rather than confrontation. They are unlikely to approach non-Chinese members of your delegation in this way. An Overseas Chinese can also check on reactions and feelings by watching their body-language. Chinese body-language is different from Western, so that you are unlikely to be able to judge what it means. Almost everything you learned on courses or from books about selling and body-language in your society does not apply outside the Western cultural framework, so that it is easy to make mistakes.

Do note, however, that Overseas Chinese have some problems unique to them. While speaking the language and being familiar with the culture, they may know little or nothing about the Chinese economy and structural/institutional networks, and you must not automatically assume they are correct in their views. It is also common for great reliance to be placed initially by you or your team on their every utterance, then later for them to be downgraded as a source when other team members have learned more. This causes a loss of face to the Overseas Chinese and places stress on them. Another problem is that if he or she has family in China, as is common, they will expect him or her to help them. As a visiting team member, this usually involves visiting them and presenting gifts. If, however, you place the Overseas Chinese permanently in China in a joint venture, etc. the expectations of the family will grow and the demands widen, e.g. for jobs. It can place the Overseas Chinese in a very difficult or impossible position.

7   Do learn a few greeting phrases, such as 'Nee haw' (How are you) or 'zummer yang' (How's it going?: only to be used when you have already broken the ice). The Chinese do not yet expect you to speak the language, but they do appreciate your attempt. A relationship develops more quickly if you demonstrate a little effort to learn even a small amount about their culture and language. Listen to how they pronounce the phrase, as Chinese is a tonal language and you should imitate the sound of the way they do it, not just learn syllables from a list.

8   Remember that face-to-face negotiations are essential. Little or nothing can be accomplished by mail or fax. A letter may not be answered and the telephone is often a source of irritation rather than a convenience. As rumours persist of telephones being bugged or operators listening to calls, you might feel that some information is better transmitted face to face in any case. You will, on occasion, find it hard to set up such a meeting; in addition to the many possible reasons, such as an important person is ill or out of town, or some meeting has to be arranged and a decision made before you can be seen, you might consider whether you have given the Chinese enough information about yourself and your company. They are often reluctant to meet unless they know a lot about you already. Supply more information at once if you suspect that this may be a factor. Once negotiations are in full swing and information is needed quickly, you can use the telephone or fax machines. The latter is best for communication, as they are more reliable and much faster than other means of communication.

9   Do try to be poised, self-controlled, and use 'soft-sell' tactics. The Chinese feel that venting frustrations in public or displaying extreme emotion is childish and thoroughly bad-mannered. They tend to have little confidence in anyone displaying emotions and do not wish to work with them. Self-control, self-discipline and calmness reap rewards. The Chinese often use the analogy of the

bamboo bending in a gale and surviving unscathed but a powerful tree like an oak snapping and falling. To succeed, you should bend with the wind, not fight it furiously.

10 Do expect to be met at an airport and at any organization you might visit. This is normal behaviour for the Chinese, and you will be escorted to where you are supposed to go. The host himself need not be on the steps to meet you, but a representative must be. As the Chinese are so status and hierarchical conscious, you can often judge how well your visit went by the rank of the person who meets you and sees you off. The level of the person meeting you shows how they rank you; the level of the person seeing you off shows how well the visit went. If the one who met you later sees you off, or, even better, if someone of higher rank does so, then you did well; if someone more junior sees you off, then your mission might be rated as not very successful.

3 Meetings and negotiations

1   Do endeavour to check that you are dealing with the appropriate organization. China is a large country and is in the process of altering from a centrally planned to a market system. Change is the order of the day, and it is not always clear what suitable organizations exist and which is the most appropriate unit to be talking to, let alone who to sign with. Once there was a handful of foreign trade corporations and that was all. Now there is a plethora of organizations at provincial and municipal level as well as Special Economic Zones, Free Trade Areas and a variety of private bodies. This is where the CCPIT and embassy assistance is useful; at least you can expect to start in an appropriate way, even if there are several bodies equally good. Your liaison middleman or help-mate should be of great assistance here. If some apparently suitable factory approaches you to do business, it just might be under the control of the wrong ministry or have low priority in the plan or be unable to obtain essential materials when required. Keep checking, as a new piece of legislation might have changed the scene or some new body might have arisen that is now more suitable for you.

2   Do note that the host organization determines your status. Your invitation to visit China will be from some organization, which is your host. The host is responsible for looking after you, including making hotel and travel bookings, and in effect vouches for you and your behaviour. A powerful host can achieve just about anything it wants, a weak one means that you can face many minor problems that irritate and waste both time and money. With the correct host you will get to places and see people that would otherwise be inaccessible to you.

3   Do approach your host organization for all requests. It is the function of your host to do everything for you, even arranging sightseeing trips, or a visit to a museum, etc. Naturally, the host

organizes your appointments with the appropriate government department or suitable private organizations.

4   Do anticipate that your host organization may not be able to make proper arrangements with other units. In principle, it should; in practice, it may not manage to do so. The 'insider–outsider' problem is involved and few organizations in China will do much to help an outsider. Your host is constantly negotiating on your behalf with other units and it is not easy to gain their cooperation. The amount of power your host has and the *guanxi* (personal relationship) it enjoys determine how successful it can be. It may also make a mistake in the complex web that is China and fail to talk to some essential organization at the periphery, so that a negotiation well under way may have to go back several steps in order to square some organization which should have been consulted earlier.

5   Do speak clearly and concisely when negotiating. It is easy for lack of communication to exist and for the Chinese side not really to understand, especially if the interpreter is not familiar with your sort of firm or business. Your own interpreter or Overseas Chinese keeping an ear open is useful to prevent such a mishap. The Chinese are likely not to admit that they do not understand (they would lose face), and in any case, often they think they understand but have an incorrect picture of what you are saying. Repeat your points using different words, and hammer home the essence of what you want to say. Good teachers have been described as those who tell you what they will say, say it, then tell you what they said. Only if your opposite number has excellent English should you not do this. Naturally, if he lived in New York for 15 years and is totally fluent, you would only annoy him – such people are, however, rare.

6   Do be punctual. It is crucial to your success to arrive for any appointment on time – aim to be early if you are able. It is the height of rudeness to keep anyone waiting. When departing your hotel, it is important to ensure that you are down in the lobby, where you meet your escort, a little early and not keep him or her waiting. Five minutes early is sufficient. If for some unavoidable reason you are late, you should apologize profusely.

7   Observe that the Chinese are patient and attentive to detail. The Chinese love details to a greater extent than in most Western societies, and do not respond easily to a 'big picture' approach unless it is backed up by many points of detail, in which case they often enjoy it. It will pay you to give your attention to

details also. It you cannot remember a fact, being able to look it up quickly is satisfactory (and see Note 23 below).

8   Appreciate that if you ask a question you may get another question in reply. This is common in Chinese culture and goes with a preference for an indirect approach and cautiously sounding out the other person without revealing too much of one's own position. This is an old negotiating ideal.

9   Do note that Chinese worry about making mistakes and being exploited. They are less nervous than during the 1970s and early 1980s, when China moved out into the international arena and had much to learn, but it is still a factor. Many delays can be attributed to these fears. They are based in part upon the historical record, for after 1840 many powerful foreign countries did use their strength to exploit China and set up colonial areas. The delays may also be caused by the slow workings of the bureaucracy. Bureaucrats the world over protect their backs.

10   Do notice that Chinese may adopt an informal approach to business outside the meetings. There is a tendency to float an idea at you in a social gathering to see how you respond. If you seem enthusiastic, it will often then be put formally at a later meeting, probably the next one. The idea is to save face in public and to ensure in principle that you are not likely to oppose the suggestion when it is made formally.

Early meetings

11   Do send your material well in advance. This gives the Chinese time to decide which institutions should be represented at the meetings with you and also for the different organizations to make the most suitable people available. They can also prepare their questions and positions in advance, which will save you time at the meetings.

12   Do learn the Chinese names before the meeting. These will normally be sent to you with the documentation. If the list is long, you should be sure you know the names of those people high on the list (see Chapter 1, Note 23). If you falter over names and misidentify people it does not endear you. Imagine how you would feel if people kept forgetting your name. It is hard at first learning foreign names, but it gets easier with practice.

13   Do expect that you will always go to a special room, which is kept solely for meetings. It is typically rather warm and furnished with soft old-fashioned sofas and chairs, and the meeting table with hard chairs around it. It looks like a period piece from a film set and is far superior to the rooms that the Chinese work in. These are so spartan and poorly equipped that special meeting rooms for entertaining visitors, especially foreigners, are essential in any institution. It is possible that further down the track, when you have developed a good relationship, you will find that you are led to a different and not quite so nice room. As decent rooms are at a premium and many people wish to meet their visitors in the best one, you might be moved down. This is not an insult, indeed it show that they have begun to like and perhaps trust you. If they make any suggestion that you could meet in your hotel, accept this, as it is easier for you with less travelling and access to your notes and records, laptop computer, etc.; the conditions are more comfortable; and the Chinese will enjoy the luxury, including being able to drink Coca-Cola, etc. This helps to put them in a happier state of mind. Try to get all such drinks or food items put on *your* bill and insist while smiling courteously. If you can manage it, you have gained an edge, in that they will feel they owe you something and will try to repay in some way that might be useful to you.

14 Do identify the leader and greet him or her first. If you are shown into an empty room, then he or she will be the first through the door. If the Chinese are waiting in the room, which is more likely, then the leader will at once acknowledge you and will in any case probably be closest to the door, or standing by the main seat in the room. As the leader of your team, you walk in first and you must greet the Chinese leader first, then the others. The Chinese will introduce them in pecking order. You then shake hands all round, unless the number is clearly excessive. You will be shown where to sit, and there is a strong protocol on this. Never just sit down without being shown where. The principal guest is usually escorted by the main host to the seat of honour. This is on the right-hand side of the host and facing the entry door. Other important guests are shown where to sit, and down at the end there may be a slight tendency to let people choose among the last few seats. The interpreter usually sits next to the host and main guest. Only after the host and guests sit down will the rest of the Chinese sit.

15 Do note that the Chinese list people in strict protocol order, as befits a hierarchical society. The leader's name will always be at the top, and the list goes down to the least important members, with the interpreters usually in last place.

16 Do observe that there is a set protocol for meetings and this will be followed. You will relax more if you know what to expect, and it is a waste of your time to try to change the format. Meetings generally begin with small talk. The first meeting, of course, starts with introductions and handshaking, and the inevitable exchange of business cards. If you lay yours out on the table in the order the Chinese are sitting, you will be able to address them by name and start to memorize faces-with-names. If someone is not introduced to you, ignore it. They might be trainee observers and too lowly to be dignified by an introduction to you. Sometimes they are Party representatives; if they look older, tough or exceptionally competent, you might suspect this to be the case.

Your aim in the early meetings is to get acquainted, not to do business. Once you have convinced them that you are the person to do business with, then things take a more Western businesslike turn. During the exchange of small talk, be careful not to appear impatient, glance at your watch or look bored. You are being closely scrutinized by all, to see if you are worthy and proper and therefore someone that they might be able to trust. The early talk will almost always be about your trip: is it your first visit, if not, how many times and where did you go, have you been to such and such a place, do you like the food, what about the weather? It is desirable to reciprocate and ask if they have had the opportunity to travelling to your country, etc.

Once the meeting starts to become a business one – leave it to the Chinese to make the switch – a set pattern follows. The leader on each side speaks in a rather formal way and the rest listen. Most hosts start with general introductions, explaining what the whole project is about, peppered with generalities and sweeping fine phrases. The Chinese are likely to leave the initiation of detailed business to you. You should first go through a polite general introduction, referring to your country and to China, to the host organization in glowing terms and to your firm, and what it can do to help. This eases you into more specific and detailed discussion. It is sometimes surprisingly hard to pin the Chinese down on what they want or are really after. You might start to suspect they do not really know, and you might be right. Be careful not to look surprised if they cannot tell you what they want. It is important to present your product, technology or case clearly and simply, and always without condescension.

Remember that each side takes turns, the leaders especially. The Chinese team members will generally not speak until their leader asks them. You might try to get your team to act like this, as the Chinese would prefer this. It is, however, not always easy to get a freewheeling group of Western business people to keep quiet. The Chinese understand this and although they might feel privately shocked at one of your team interrupting you, their leader, they will not be particularly surprised. Be careful not to interrupt them, of course, as this would be most rude and cause of loss of face. It is equally important not to press anyone for information they are not giving you, such as who is really responsible for the decision or what the shipping tonnage available really is. If you need to know and they are being coy, you can try asking them to consider it later and see if they can find out for you. That allows them to agree and takes them off the hook. They might indeed deliver the information later, once this has been approved.

17 Do read their business card slowly and carefully. In China, a person is identified by which firm they work for, and after that by their position within the firm. You might even hear a Chinese say 'I am IBM', by which they mean, of course, that they work for IBM, but this specifies that they are in a major foreign firm and hence someone of importance. It helps to classify them in the hierarchy and in a sense the card is an extension of themselves. To glance at a card and put it immediately in your pocket is discourteous in China and is an insult, signifying that you consider they are not worth bothering about. It is particularly bad to place a card in your back trouser pocket where it will be sat on, as the symbolism is not lost on the Chinese, even if unintended by you. Read the card carefully, look at the person and smile and nod, then place all cards in front of you on the table. If you are in an armchair, it is acceptable to put them on the arm.

18 Three-hour meetings are common in China, often starting at 9 am, with perhaps a two or two-and-a-half hour lunch break, then reconvening, if necessary, around 2 or 2.30 pm for a further three hours. It can be tiring for foreigners who are not used to this. Business meetings in the West are often kept as short as possible. In China, time is not particularly regarded as money, nor as something that must be carefully used, so that meetings can drag on in an interminable way. Decades of sitting through political meetings that could literally last for days, with breaks for sleep, have trained many Chinese to endure sessions that resemble filibusters.

19 You can expect to drink lots of tea without milk and sugar during meetings, poured by service personnel (not 'servants') from vacuum flasks. Be careful not to overdo it and strain your bladder. You can also expect to listen to bland introductions, often full of happy platitudes. Be prepared to deliver similar speeches that sound mundane but mean a lot in the context of Chinese culture.

20 Anticipate that the first and next few early meetings will be formal and that business will go slowly. In later meetings you will often find that the Chinese will move about, talk among themselves and leave and re-enter the room. This is not impolite in China, and you should not take offence, or even obviously note their behaviour.

21 An important reason for putting up calmly with the early meetings and lack of progress is that the Chinese start to assess you at once. The early meetings are designed for the purpose of gauging what you are like, and examining you for weaknesses such as impatience, lack of self-control or inability to cope with long sessions. This information will be used to their advantage in the later negotiating process. Naturally, you should be doing the same and probing for weakness, but on their playing field and with their rules, you are at a disadvantage. Additionally, like most Asians, the Chinese are only happy doing business with someone they know and trust, and this takes time. The meetings are a part of the process of mutual learning.

22 Try to listen carefully in the early meetings, even when assaulted by platitudes. You might get hints and ideas about what the Chinese really want, for they will probably not come out openly and tell you, especially until time has passed and they know you better.

23 It is vital that you take careful notes of what is discussed as well as decided. It is possible that misunderstandings will arise and one side think that X is decided, another Y. More commonly, one side thinks that X was decided, the other side thinks it was merely discussed and left in the air. If you have notes to refer to, you can counter suggestions that something you did not agree to should be done. Producing your original notes is usually enough to persuade the Chinese that you are serious as well as aware. Some Chinese negotiators might try it on, to see if they can talk you into thinking you agreed to something earlier. They might also try to instill a feeling of guilt and embarrass you into agreeing to something they say you accepted earlier.

24 Do take your own interpreter if possible. It is reasonably common for leading Chinese to speak English but rare for them to negotiate in the language. Expect that all business will be transacted in Chinese. An interpreter is necessary and the Chinese will supply one who will translate accurately enough. However, you should seriously consider bringing your own interpreter with you, as this has several advantages. If you are negotiating a deal or agreement that contains complicated legal or business ideas, or has a mass of details, you can brief your own interpreter before you leave your own country and make sure that he or she understands what you want and what the concepts actually mean. This can prevent a lot of misunderstanding. Your own interpreter can choose to soften or select the best phrase to put over your perhaps blunt point or correct the name if you get it wrong, whereas their interpreter has nothing to gain from doing so, other than perhaps avoiding feeling embarrassed. Like an Overseas Chinese team member, your own interpreter can also tell you what they are saying among themselves, watch their body-language, check that they really do understand and provide a route for indirect communications. Conventionally, with your own interpreter, he or she translates what you say, and the Chinese-supplied one translates what they say.

If you cannot take an interpreter with you, then you should make a list of all the technical terms that you think might be used and get them properly translated before going to China. You could usefully send a copy of the list to the Chinese side before you leave, to allow their translators to brush up in these areas.

Checking on the standard of interpretation is not too difficult. If you are puzzled by what their interpreter says to you, or if you get an answer that does not fit the question you asked, then you have reason to be concerned about the interpretation. Similarly, if they look puzzled or keep discussing what the technical terms really mean, then your interpreter may not be doing well. Be watchful for people who are not interpreters interjecting a translation – it means that they see that the interpreter is mistranslating and are correcting him or her. As this means a loss of face to the interpreter, they will usually only do this if the mistranslation is a serious one. If you listen to five minutes of Chinese and get a 'No, it is not possible' then you know you are getting a poor translation. If you give any figures or statistics and the interpreter does not immediately seize a pencil and write the figures on a piece of paper, suspect that he or she is not really good. As China has a different counting system over 1000 – it goes to 10 000 rather than to a million, then proceeds in lots of 10 000s – it is hard to translate large numbers without writing them down.

   If you have brought a poor interpreter then that is your fault and you must live with it. If the Chinese supplied a poor one, then it is hard but not impossible to ask for a different one. It is a difficult matter, for it is a serious criticism of the interpreter and will cause an extreme loss of face for him or her. Consider also that you might get an even worse one as a replacement, as good English interpreters are in short supply in China, and there is a big demand for their services.

25 Do use the interpreter properly to gain the maximum benefit. When negotiating, do not address the interpreter but look at the person you are really addressing, which is usually their leader. Use short sentences and pause often. Try to get a rhythm of saying perhaps one or two sentences, then stopping. The interpreter will pick up this rhythm and work better, smoothly stepping in on time, and not interrupting or losing track of what you are saying. If the interpreter ever interrupts you, it means that you are speaking in too big chunks without a pause. Naturally, you should not raise your voice if translations are apparently going badly; just keep saying the same thing but in different ways. It is, in any case, a good idea to say any important matters twice, but choosing quite different words, as the message is more certain of getting across.

26 Observe that in all negotiations the Chinese prefer to start with general principles, and only move to details later. Notice that the early stated and agreed principles are more than ritual statements and that this stage is not a waste of time. You should think carefully about the principles before accepting them, for when you agree to a general principle you accept it for all time. You should note that the approach is the exact opposite to that in the West, where it is thought that a general agreement is best obtained by focusing on specific details within a known and accepted legal framework. You will find that contracts and agreements come later, only after the generalities have been settled. Note that a 'letter of intent' or 'memorandum of understanding' is not a contract in the Western sense, and has no legal force. It is in such a document that the agreed general principles are expressed.

Why do the Chinese place so much emphasis on general principles? It is partly a matter of cultural tradition, but there are some practical advantages for China. The Chinese are adept at using the principles to increase the pressure when negotiating and they may choose words that might allow them to wring later concessions. They are engaged in assessing if you are reliable and sincere, as well as the proper person/firm with which to do business. They are also weighing up your vulnerability and degree of persistence. Some of the general principles being promoted might be on orders from above and hence cannot be dropped or altered without approval. If at this stage you are asked to reveal detailed information that appears to have commercial value and which you do not want to give away, you might be able to put them off by pointing out that such matters are best considered later, when details will be discussed.

In both political and business negotiations it is quite common to be accused of violating the agreed principles and the spirit of the earlier agreement. The Chinese are clever at trying to shame their opponents into agreeing, and this is a traditional Chinese negotiating practice. They take shame very seriously, both for themselves and for others. On the other hand, you can play the same game, and if you appeal to the general agreed principles, you might find that the Chinese will give up a particular demand more easily.

The emphasis on general ethical and moral principles that shows in early negotiations has a long history in China and the Chinese prefer ethical principles to the law or recourse to the courts (see Chapter 5, Note 21).

27 Do note that Chinese may see problems differently. Many Western business people have two main corporate goals: to make (increase) profit and to maintain (increase) market share. The Chinese may have more aims. They are more aware of the nation and its efforts, and may wish China to modernize, to grow and become strong, which may override any thought of profits. They also have to cope with more fear and intrigue than many Westerners, and have been trained to be cautious, often by being forcibly sent to do manual work, moved to remote country areas, or perhaps even tortured and imprisoned during the Cultural Revolution or other political movements of the past.

Many Western business people see their career as a sort of sport, where they try to win both personally and for their organization by playing against opponents under more or less set rules.

When the contract is signed, the first half is over; when the goods are delivered or project complete, the whole game is over and a new one has to start. For the Chinese, business negotiations are more complex, and while the sport analogy has relevance, the process is also like a marriage, perhaps an arranged one, where the relationship starts off in ignorance of the other but steadily grows and develops if the choice of partner was correct.

4 Meetings and negotiations – your tactics

1   Do recall that you are working for a long-term relationship. The Chinese approach negotiation not merely to sign a contract but to develop a relationship which will last and, hopefully, lead to more business over the years. Westerners often have a shorter focus than this and you must beware of letting the Chinese think that you are not in it for the long term. You are striving for an 'in-depth relationship' and becoming 'an old friend'.

2   Do note that negotiations can take a long time. As a result of being involved in long and tedious talks, some Westerners have felt that the Chinese would rather negotiate than do a deal! There are many possible reasons for delays. Among them may be that your host company is a weak one that does not have the power to secure what it and you want. It may be inexperience on their part, although this may be reducing. It may be that several different bureaucratic bodies are involved and mutual agreement cannot be reached, perhaps because of power boundary disputes, or because scarce assets will need transferring to another authority, which few are willing to do. All organs guard their possessions jealously and refuse to help another unless forced to by higher levels. Other reasons for delays may be that someone who has to approve the idea is sick or has gone abroad for a time and nothing can happen until their return; insecurity and fear that the leader or someone on the Chinese side might be criticized; or a Chinese fear that you might exploit them so they are gathering information internationally about you, the product or technology which takes time. In addition, it is possible that the Chinese have begun to negotiate with a rival firm of yours and are comparing your proposition with theirs. There is a shortage of interpreters and yours might have been suddenly allocated to another set of meetings so that your group is unable to meet and negotiate. Delays during negotiations might also be induced as a

deliberate tactic, if the Chinese feel that you are an impatient person or are eager to return to your own country. They can perhaps pressure you into accepting more of their demands that way. You should accept that you might have to leave without an agreement, but if this looks like a possibility, you can warn them that it will probably be some time before you can return to China, which will return the pressure.

3   Do expect the bureaucracy to be slow and not always helpful. China is a huge country and communications have always been poor. A giant bureaucracy ran China and held it together as a nation for at least 2000 years. With that kind of history and experience each unit, whether a factory or ministry, looks after its own interests first. With the traditional 'insider–outsider' differences, no unit ever willingly helps another and many will actively hinder others. This situation means that there is a great use of *quanxi* (a network of relationships) and contacts, and therefore you should try to do favours for people as they in turn must repay you in some way.

4   Do expect to encounter rivalry between organizations. These are not coordinated horizontally and all requests and orders simply go up and down. When dealing with China, it is crucial to ascertain which other bodies will have an interest in the project and to make sure that either they are involved in the meetings or the deal is being communicated to them. Some projects have been held up for lengthy periods because no one secured the cooperation of the electricity-supply authority or the like. If you are established in China and apply to do something different, e.g. produce a different item, and should the item come under the control of a different authority, the local people are more likely than not to oppose the idea, even if it is a good one. They see that the benefits will go elsewhere, not to their unit.

5   Do expect marathon negotiations with little rest. There is a mixture of reasons for this. Traditionally, China sees keeping an opponent active and allowing no rest as a valuable part of warfare. Business is sometimes seen as an extension of war by other means. If in your case the Chinese side sees the negotiations in an adversarial way, then they may try to wear you down. Sudden switches from going slow to going fast, then finding a reason for delays, are a familiar story in Chinese history. Cunning is valued when pitted against a superior and formal force, rather like the Robin Hood myths familiar in Britain and America. China is a poor country and those working there are used to

long days and six-day working weeks. You may not be, and are more likely to become tired as a result. Further, under Mao, they learned to endure long meetings and still stay awake and concentrating for their own safety. They really are good in this regard.

6   Do be patient, polite and dignified, and avoid rudeness. You will need patience in negotiations as well as in adapting to the slower pace of living in China. Everything takes time, items ordered can take ages to arrive, and apparently simple requests can disappear into the bureaucracy for what seems to be eternity. It might take months or even years in China, as well as several trips, to achieve what you wish. Even then you may be hit with a request to renegotiate something that has already been decided. Politeness is a virtue, as is human dignity, and you should strive to achieve both. Withdrawn, quiet behaviour is valued; slapping people on the back, putting your arm around their shoulders, or engaging in 'big' behaviour is anathema to the Chinese, as to most Asians. It is wise to avoid informing them when you must leave China, as if you do, nothing might occur for some time, then a day or two before you intend to leave you might be given a well-designed proposal that does not exactly favour you but which it is tempting to sign.

Try to be soft and gentle, courteous and considerate. It is polite to be humble or appear to be so, even if you are pretending. Whenever someone says they are not good enough at doing something or in their job, it is merely a polite formula and not to be believed. You should reply that they clearly are very good in that area. True emotions are concealed in Chinese culture, so that pretence is not regarded as two-faced or deceitful in the way it might be in some Western countries. Manners are separated from feelings.

7   You should always be honest and sincere, and tell the truth. The Chinese make a practice of checking up on people and their statements and there is no shortage of personnel to do this. The Chinese tend to be suspicious, as a result of their treatment in history as well as some more recent rather outrageous events after foreigners were allowed in quantity to do business. If you are found to have lied, your business will not be wanted, or else you may have to make major concessions in order to continue.

8   Do persevere and persist; China can be a good market but it is not easy. Gentle persistence is needed. If the Chinese really want to deal, they might suddenly offer major concessions (after you have informed them of the date you will leave) on your very last day and sign quickly.

9   Do be very careful not to cause a loss of face. Each person has a role to play in a group and causing someone to lose face means that everyone in the group is aware of the incident and may personally feel let down. The entire group is likely to respond badly to you henceforth. It is not always easy to determine what might cause a loss of face; criticizing someone in public is an obvious one, as is ignoring the Chinese leader and addressing someone else in the Chinese team, or these days giving a present that is too cheap (see Note 24 below).

Conversely, giving face to someone is excellent. Anything that boosts ego is good, e.g. praising someone or going out of your way to do something for someone. Dealing with a large international firm gives face to a Chinese firm, which is one reason they prefer the biggest and best. A good reason for taking an Overseas Chinese with you if possible is that the Chinese will make suggestions to them which allows them to save face if the idea does not go ahead. It often seems in China that face is more important than honesty. A Chinese would often prefer to tell you a lie than the truth, when the latter would cause you to lose face. If you ask to see a building and are informed that it 'closed', it often means that there is some reason why you should not be allowed to see it. For example, some churches during the Cultural Revolution were taken for use as warehouses and the Chinese did not want foreigners to know this.

10   Do try to do small favours and develop a relationship. Partly this gives face but, more importantly, favours must be repaid and all Chinese officials and business people, as well as people in their ordinary life, work in a network of favours owed and owing. Anything you want to acquire or get done tends to be facilitated by going through this network. Without such a network very little can be achieved. For the Chinese a relationship can be built on such things as a shared background in a province, or having been to the same school, even if miles or years apart (see Chapter 1, Note 9). For you as a foreigner, a relationship is harder to develop but can be built on shared experiences, having both visited a certain country, having the same hobby, having the same number of children of the same sex or having done business together before. It is tenuous but it is a start. The easiest way is to hire the son or daughter of a powerful local official to work for you. This tends to open many doors.

11   Do treat bureaucrats sympathetically. Some have immense power and it will probably not be apparent to you who wields real power or even who is responsible for what area. If you offend someone with power, a series of things can go badly for you without apparent cause.

12 When negotiating, do give the shortest reply possible. The more you say, the more you might tend to make concessions or reveal a lever that the Chinese will pounce upon and use. They also tend to distrust big talkers and fast-pitch sales people, having had some bad experiences with such types. Save your long speeches for introductions and the start of meetings, and make them flowery, general and full of what you might think of as banal statements, as these tend to reassure the Chinese.

13 Do look for a concealed 'no'. The Chinese dislike saying 'no' to people as they feel that it causes the recipient a loss of face. They seek other ways to say no, including 'Possibly', 'Maybe' or 'It might be possible'. If they say 'It will be difficult' you are usually hearing a straight 'no', as you are if they look in consternation at each other before saying 'Maybe' or 'We will try', 'It is not convenient' or 'There is no responsible person'. Even 'We will think about it' often means 'no', as do phrases like 'This is the first request of this kind we have had', or 'The matter is under consideration' (although this may be genuine). If you make a request, or write a letter, and get no reply, that also means a polite 'no'. Body-language can reveal a 'no', for example a sharp waving motion of the hand across the front of the face, or sucking in breath between clenched teeth before speaking. Even silence in reply to your question often indicates 'no'.

14 Do look for indirect signals. Much in Chinese society is done indirectly, avoiding all possibility of confrontation. Any unpalatable truths are best done through an intermediary if possible. Signals such as body-language abound, but you should be aware that if nothing seems to be happening it may be a signal in itself. Observe that if the Chinese continually push for something that seems outrageous, you might be getting the signal that they wish to stop negotiations and are trying to force you to break them off. If you are faced with this situation, it helps to say you will report back to headquarters (if you are not a one-person firm) and consider it, as this keeps the negotiations open. A blunt 'no' should be avoided if you can, unless you have decided to cut your losses and leave.

15 Do enquire after China's problems that may be relevant to your firm and products. Asking about national priorities, the current five-year plan, and local needs and current development projects

shows interest, gives good topics of conversation, and might reveal areas in which you can do business. The Chinese have a habit of not saying exactly what the problems are or what they really want, but leaving it to you to offer things. Knowing the general areas of local development and interest is a start for you.

16   Do keep a written list of your goals and expected costs of both items and processes and be aware of the value of intangibles and your know-how. The Chinese do not seem to place a money value on much information that in the West carries a price tag. They might want a lot of intangible items free, so be aware of what it will cost to bundle in overseas visits, free manuals, technical training seminars, etc. and include it in your price. As negotiations are normally done item by item, if you concede things early on, you may lose track of the accumulating promises, so keep good notes. Otherwise the final cost of what you have agreed might surprise you. Be prepared to face close questioning on how you arrive at a price for intangible items.

17   Do set your price to allow some leeway. Pricing is not easy. If you set it too low, then additional requests, often after the contract has been signed, might eat away all the profit. If too high, then you will not be competitive and the Chinese will probably know this as they check international prices carefully. You should try to get the agreement on prices flexible for the future, as changes might occur that force up your costs. Be particularly careful not to specify a price early in negotiations as a little leeway does help, since you will have something to bargain with if extra demands are made.

18   Do keep repeating your needs clearly. The Chinese may not fully understand what you want and repetition does no harm. More usually, a problem with obtaining things is caused by the bureaucratic system and lack of horizontal coordination. You should keep pressing quietly for what you need. Requests often have to be raised several times before action occurs and you might find that you have to hound them. While waiting, you can use the time to do something else. You might find it worthwhile to keep a list of things that you can do when left to your own devices.

19   At the end of a meeting do summarize what has been agreed. It is commonplace that one side believes that something has been agreed but the other thinks that it was merely discussed then put aside. At the end of each meeting it is a valuable habit to sum up what has been agreed, what the next action will be, and who will take it, so that both sides know where they stand. It helps if you can establish who among the Chinese will be your contact person so that you can keep in touch.

20 Do note that it is easy to misjudge how well negotiations are proceeding. This is the result of several factors. China is very different from Western societies, the bureaucracy is vast and unfathomable even for most Chinese, and much information that would be public knowledge in the West is kept secret. Further, the Chinese negotiators may not know what their superiors really think, and so do not know how seriously they should tackle things. In addition, some foreigners have difficulty in reading Chinese features and the body-language is different, so that misinterpretations can easily occur. Also, Chinese negotiators tend to deal either at the level of global and rather bland generalities (friendship between our two nations, etc.) or else with specific and concrete matters of detail. Neither level reveals much about the rate of progress being achieved. You usually lack experience in dealing in that province and with that particular team, so that what is 'normal' is not clear to you. You might find things go slowly, then suddenly speed up; or you might feel things are progressing well, but really not much is happening. If the Chinese suddenly want publicity, it is often a signal that the end is in sight. But be careful that they are not encouraging you to go public with broad details of the agreement merely to increase the pressure on you to concede important details. They are well aware that you will wish to conclude the agreement rather than back out once it has been well publicized.

21 Do consider using a 'go-between' to transmit bad news. This avoids you having to say 'no' personally, but the message gets across. China has always done this – during Mao Zedong's reign of power the ever-popular Zhou Enlai was often used to break bad news, such as major harvest failures, to the people in order to preserve Mao's position. Your local agent might function for you here.

22 The Chinese will usually press hard to gain the maximum concession and should you be pushed back to your minimum position, stand firm. Be prepared to walk away from negotiating if necessary. It is usually better to do this and cut your losses than to accept a deal that will cost you money. The only exception is if your company is large enough to take a long-term view and hope for future gains to offset initial losses. Many Western firms have done this and while eventually they may make profits, these are frequently insufficient to offset the earlier losses, particularly if the trouble and elapsed time involved are considered. If you see an encouraging survey of profitable foreign firms in China it might tend to gloss over this fact, for few business people like to admit to mistakes. Keep in mind that there are markets other than China where money can be made.

23   Be aware that the Chinese usually want the latest technology rather than seeking to preserve jobs (see Chapter 1, Note 12). This is despite having a huge population. It is also common to meet a rather naive belief that modern technology will solve all their problems. This erroneous view has a long history in China and was very popular in the last half of the nineteenth century.

24   You should take a lot of gifts with you to China but choose them carefully. Gifts fall into two kinds, those to delegations or teams and those to individuals. Gifts also have several functions: (1) they show esteem and liking; (2) they are to repay a favour or gain the chance of a favour, either now or in the future; (3) they are mementos; and (4) they are expected in certain social situations, such as when invited to visit a home.

Gifts from your team to the Chinese side are of two kinds. There may be one large gift that really goes to the institution itself and a small gift that is given to each individual member of the Chinese team. The large gift could be a memento of your company, a 'coffee table' book that is related in some way to your or their area of interest (e.g. ports of the world to a shipping company) or something similar. If a book, ensure that your company chairman or high official has inscribed it; this shows respect and impresses. Try to get your logo on if possible. Small gifts are mementos only and should be inexpensive. Chinese teams abroad may give a tie pin, etc. costing a few pence. It is the thought rather than the value that counts. Small, cheap electronic devices such as a calculator are prized items. Your supermarket and cut-price shops back home have many small cheap items that are often unobtainable in China and hence highly prized. If your company has cheap plastic briefcases or the like with your logo on, they would make a very acceptable present. They should not be too expensive, however. Take lots of presents – Chinese teams of up to a dozen are common, and you might deal with more than one team. Everyone involved gets a present, including the interpreters and a regular driver should get one too. Drivers are very important people in China and can have much power. It is better not to wrap up any of these small gifts, but if you do so, never use white paper and try not to have them in a white paper bag.

If you wish to make a gift to someone on a personal basis, it is best done in private. A bottle of foreign spirits is fine (brandy is often preferred to whisky by Overseas Chinese but in China there so far seems little preference). Good foreign chocolates are also acceptable, as is a carton of cigarettes. The brand 'Three Fives' is often preferred and is used as a trading good, so non-smokers also accept them happily. Other good gifts are cigarette lighters, pens, small portable electronic devices (it is a good idea to supply a spare battery as these may be hard/impossible to get locally), or something typical of and made in your own country.

If a Chinese is offered a gift, it is polite to refuse up to three times, so when offering the gift, do persist, smiling and gesturing. If you hear the word repeated rapidly three times as 'No, no, no' they might actually mean it. Hold the gift in both hands, as this is polite. One-handed gifts show a lack of respect. You will find that Westernized or well-travelled Chinese will usually offer gifts to foreigners with one hand, as they have learned our customs too, but among themselves, two-handed is polite. They notice every time you do it and know that you understand something of the culture.

If invited to visit a Chinese home, probably for a meal, you must take a gift with you. Exotic fresh fruit is nice, if you can find some locally, perhaps in your hotel. You can hardly bring some in on the off-chance of needing it. Spirits, chocolates, and books in the English language are also very acceptable. Someone in the family is almost certain to be studying English. Perfume and cologne are much prized, but aftershave is less used, because Chinese shave rather infrequently. You should compliment the host on the house, the furnishings generally and especially the food, but not any particular item. You might be shocked at the low standard of living enjoyed by some powerful people, but if so, you should hide it. Do eat heartily, as it shows that you are enjoying yourself, but leave something on the communal plate if the wife is not eating with you – she will probably eat the leftovers later (and see Chapter 6, Note 4 for table manners). Reciprocate the invitation and invite them to a meal at your hotel or in a good local restaurant.

If you wrap a gift, the family may not open it at once but wait until you leave, which is a common Chinese practice. If you wish, you can explain it is the custom in your country to open it at once and they will often take the hint. Do not press it, of course. Remember not to ask for a drink, as this would insult the host, who should watch you and keep your glass full. You will probably eat early, perhaps 6.30 pm or so, and finish by 8 or 8.30 pm. If you make noises about leaving about half an hour after the meal, it will be appreciated.

Tipping, once forbidden, has crept back into China. If you wish to tip your waiter, etc. in the hotel, do it quietly and, if you can do so, in private. A small gift that can be slipped into a pocket is often more acceptable than money as there may be not much to buy in the shops that the person wants or does not already have, whereas small imported items are often totally unavailable and hence prized. What seems a cheap plastic or glass 'novelty' item in London, New York, or Sydney can be highly esteemed in China.

25 Do accept that you may need to invite the Chinese to visit your country or pay for a local trip for the Chinese. If you represent a large company you should accept that you may have to invite a small number of Chinese to visit your country at your expense. While this is ostensibly a business-familiarization trip, you might find that they rapidly wish to go sightseeing, to Disneyland, a Movie-World, an Oceanarium and the like. If you are a small firm, then you might be expected to pay for a domestic trip for the Chinese, perhaps to a local holiday area or to Beijing.

26 Do send the same personnel each time if possible. They rapidly acquire the status of 'old friends' and it avoids the problem of forcing the Chinese to start to assess a new person which would involve delays. 'Old friends' are valued by the Chinese and they make much of the concept. There is a long history of poetry focused on the value of friendship. The Chinese approach of dividing the world into 'insiders' and 'outsiders' accentuates the value of being a friend. Developing an easy and close relationship is of crucial importance to doing business in China. Being a friend is part of this process and you should strive to build friendship with people in any unit you deal with. Yet there is an element of ritual about being called an 'old friend', and sometimes it may just be something to say which is not inappropriate and that sounds nice. It can also be an effort to raise the status of the person saying it or even be a bargaining ploy to try to gain concessions from you. As the Chinese often use the phrase when there is nothing to be gained, you should not automatically assume that it is a simple ploy.

An 'old friend' can be someone who has been to China before and is an old friend of China, even if he or she is not personally known to the person. Of course, it is far better if someone is known personally. When told you are an old friend it is polite to deny it and say something along the lines of you know very little about the complex and marvellous country.

The Chinese do expect a well-off friend to do favours and might disappointedly accuse you of not following the spirit of the agreement signed earlier if you refuse, for example, to supply free technical seminars. Friendship implies obligations and friends should not keep secrets from each other. As most Chinese do not quickly or easily make close friends with foreigners, the claim to friendship is usually not genuine in a Western sense, but note that it may be genuine in the Chinese sense, in that it shows that the relationship has started to be built.

27 In general terms, expect to be treated rather like a supplicant to a powerful emperor from a weak tributary state. This is the old model of China's relationship with the world and things have not changed much. The Chinese know they are the best and have the best culture and history, but feel that they have been dogged by an inability to modernize and cope with the impact of foreigners since the mid-nineteenth century.

28 Do send a senior person to conclude negotiations. If this is done when the negotiations are at an advanced stage it raises the quality of the agreement in Chinese eyes and they are likely to treat it in a more important way. Status is extremely important in the culture, which is often difficult for people from more egalitarian and perhaps recently settled countries such as North America and Australia both to notice and accept. After the signing, the senior representative should host a dinner to celebrate the signing and not just leave China.

Note that during negotiations, the Chinese may themselves suddenly produce a senior person and thrust him or her at you. They may do this as a tactic in order to try to wring an important concession from you, or it may indicate that they are taking the negotiations more seriously and may have upgraded the priority of the project.

5 Meetings and negotiations – their tactics

1   The Chinese prefer to negotiate in China rather than abroad. They gain advantages from this, for as host they set the agenda and pace of negotiations, and can adjust these if they can see something to be gained. They can easily send large numbers to learn from you cheaply if during the negotiations they can persuade you to give a free demonstration or training seminar. During negotiations they also have back-up staff easily available and can check with higher levels more conveniently. As everything in China must be approved by someone higher up, this is a matter of great importance to them. Conversely, you are at a disadvantage, cut off as you are from your own society and firm, probably suffering from culture shock as well as being tired, and lacking back-up staff.

    Chinese delegations abroad are often window-shopping and gaining information on different rival products and areas, rather than seriously negotiating. Such trips abroad are commonly used as pay-offs for favours done, and little or no business may eventuate from some trips. Even where the visit is a serious one intending to do business, some people are probably there as a pay-back and there is no guarantee that they were the best person to be sent. 'Buggin's turn' also operates in China and some are sent who have little or nothing to contribute. Irrespective of whether the trip is a genuine one or not, all decisions will be made in China. Despite the problems involved with Chinese visits, it is customary to invite your Chinese host to come to your country (you will, of course, pay).

2   When you are in China, do expect to face a large Chinese team. The Chinese often field a team of eight to twelve people, including the leader, some engineers and technicians, a few sales or purchasing people, and several others who may not have any obvious function. Some may be trainees, others Party representatives, one may have an intelligence function, there may be a lawyer, or someone visiting the area from higher up the ladder. The team will rarely be united in view, as the main negotiator wants the lowest price, the engineers the best product/technology to solve a problem, different end-users might want different things, while any local financial representative will probably wish to minimize total expenditure of either money or foreign exchange. Further, different members of the team will be reporting to different authorities, which complicates matters. Despite this, as far as you are concerned, the Chinese team functions as a unit and maintains accord in public.

Do note that an apparently unimportant Chinese team member can have a major influence on decisions. The leader in fact may not be the person present with the most power, and the really important person present may rarely (if ever) speak. Should any previously silent person interrupt one of his own team, especially the leader, you may assume that their power is great. Above the team there is a bureaucratic ladder of people most of whom possess more power than the leader opposite you.

3   You should discount enthusiastic Chinese statements about future prospects or their own power and ability to influence outcomes. In the early stages of negotiation, the Chinese tend to exaggerate China's potential and huge market. While China has grown rapidly and it currently looks as if this will continue in the immediate future, it is a difficult, if rewarding, market. You should be aware that the negotiator may exaggerate his or her power to make decisions in order to impress. Later you might find that meetings are deferred or closed early, in order to obtain instructions from higher levels. Potential help-mates may also exaggerate their connections and closeness to central power in order to get work from you.

4   You will probably find that after the preliminary statements are over, you, the visitor, will be expected to reveal your position first. This can be difficult, as it is not always clear what the Chinese really want or what are the main problems for which they seek a solution. They are even less inclined to reveal their priorities about problems to you. To an extent, you will be groping in the dark. In this process you might inadvertently reveal more than you would wish.

The Chinese then react to your presentation. At this early stage they may try to get you to promise more than is reasonable or than you can deliver. As they take copious notes and have good memories, any concession you indicate might be possible, may re-emerge later as something you promised.

5   The Chinese are constantly engaged in seeking out your weaknesses and trying to ascertain if you are greedy, impatient, remember details or forget them, drink a lot and forget what you said and so on. This scrutiny occurs outside meetings too, e.g. at social events. At the early stage, small baits may be dangled in front of you in order to encourage you to continue negotiating, and for them to gain something from you, such as free information. Expect the Chinese to try to get you to exaggerate your capabilities and take care.

Your body-language will be scrutinized closely for signs of impatience, anger, relaxation, things that please you, and so forth. The Chinese are happier with silence than many Westerners and do not feel the need to jump in and break it. You might find that early in the meetings they sit in silence and observe how you react, looking to see if it puts pressure on you and if it could be used as a weapon later. Some signals will be misinterpreted across the cultures, but they have gained much experience of dealing with Westerners. The information obtained in these ways will be used in deciding what approaches are likely to be the most advantageous to maximize the concessions that can be wrung from you.

6   As negotiators, the Chinese stress mutual interests, rather than compromise, and flowery rhetoric can abound. In fact they feel that in negotiations there are winners and losers, and they try very hard to win. Losing also causes a loss of face. Expect to find that if you negotiate a hard bargain and 'win', the Chinese will re-open issues previously decided, to try to improve their position. It is normal to be asked for special treatment for China, which is poor, and trying to catch up when compared with your wealthy developed country. You might be told that China was treated badly by certain Western countries in the past and the world 'owes' China something. You should, of course, avoid feeling a sense of personal shame or guilt if your country has acted in this way or if it is fortunate enough to be wealthy.

The Chinese genuinely believe that once mutual interest has been established, the richer party should do more for the poorer and tend to expect that Westerners should take non-monetary rewards. After decades of being scorned, profit is now accepted as a reasonable thing, but there is often a Marxist hangover that fears profits, especially large ones, and denounces greed.

Traditionally, the Chinese have seen their country as special, and one that merits especially favourable treatment. They still do. Surprisingly, some otherwise hard-headed Western business people often accept this view too.

7   Do expect major issues to be raised on social occasions. The Chinese never stop negotiating and a laughing concession made by you while drinking at a banquet is likely to appear at the next meeting as a settled issue.

8   Do expect to be played off against competitors. Chinese negotiators have few scruples about revealing information gained in negotiations with one company to pressure another to make concessions. Clearly if a 'round' of competing offers can be established, this can be profitable for China. You may be told that a competing Western firm has given them the information about something, so you should do the same, or perhaps the competitor has already offered a better deal than the one you propose. This may or may not be true.

9   Do note that time and money are quite separate concepts in China. Westerners tend to regard time as money; few Chinese do this. In addition, labour in China is cheap, so that if someone spends much time on a task, it actually does not cost much. These are two reasons why negotiations can drag on interminably, for the time spent is regarded as a free good. If running a joint venture in China, you are likely to come across this attitude to time and find a Chinese manager undertaking tasks that would be bought in from outside in a Western country.

Labour may, however, cost you more than you think, for workers are often paid a much higher wage than they actually receive. The government takes the difference, which can exceed the amount received. This reduces the benefit of being in China for the low wages and if you are an internationally footloose firm, other venues might be worth considering. In any case, low wages do not always equal low costs, it all depends on the productivity of labour. Chinese labour does not enjoy notably high levels of productivity, although it has improved over the last decade.

10   Observe that the Chinese may see negotiations differently from you. Many Asians have a different attitude to life from those raised in a Western culture. Rather than focusing on cause and effect, as in most Western societies, they envisage the world as a complex pattern, like a web, with links sideways as well as backwards and forwards in place and time. Life is a stream, a flowing process. If asked why something has happened they are inclined to interpret the problem in those terms. It is thus often difficult for them to explain something to Westerners and for the latter to understand, because of the difference in approach. A solution proposed by the Chinese may not seem to you to attack the root cause, just as a solution proposed by you might seem unsatisfactory to a Chinese as, although it may attack the cause, it may upset an established pattern and hence be undesirable. It might also offend some outside organization that would then try to sabotage the deal. Negotiations sometimes appear differently to each side as a result of such different world-views.

11   Do anticipate that the Chinese will keep returning to and raising old issues. When this happens, be patient and smile. Partly it is a fascination with detail and many Chinese can cope endlessly with it without seemingly getting bored. They tend to dislike carelessness about the fine points. Vast amounts of detail might be required, which is why a knowledgeable engineer is a valuable member of your team. Partly it is a tactic, as in Chinese eyes details can always be renegotiated.

12   Do expect Chinese to wander in and out during talks, as this is not considered rude. They will not normally do this in the early stages when they are feeling formal and stilted, so that if you observe it, it shows that they are relaxing. Knowing this can help you in negotiations as you can judge how fast the relationship is developing.

13   Do observe that *guanxi* (personal 'pull' with people in a relationship) is much used. The Chinese have a habit of spinning a web of dependency and using it for their ends. As they are expert in this area and you are probably not, it is hardly surprising that they are often successful here. The relationship should be two-way, of course, and you should also use the relationship to try to obtain what you need. *Guanxi,* the name of such relationships, means you can call upon special help and favours which must be given even if it disadvantages the giver. Any favour must be repaid in turn at some stage. The bank account of favours is not unlimited, so after receiving, say, two favours, a person definitely must repay when asked. You should try to develop such connections for success in China.

14   Do note the importance of symbols. In general, the Chinese prefer to have the most prestigious brand or technology, even if it is not the most suitable (see Chapter 1, Notes 12 and 14 and Chapter 4, Note 23). If yours is not the leader, you must be careful not to stress that it is much cheaper, but try to show that it is actually better in some way (and more suitable is not necessarily better). Similarly, the Chinese find it hard to reject a symbolic gesture that appeals to the general principles agreed earlier, even if it is not what they want. They will usually feel obliged to reciprocate the gesture in some way.

15 Do expect the truth to be a flexible commodity. Traditionally, the Chinese have not found the truth to be an overwhelmingly important criterion. It was widely accepted that if it was in one's interest to tell the truth, then it was sensible to do so, otherwise not. Partly as a result of this, the law courts regularly used torture in an effort to get at the truth. In contemporary times, this traditional attitude has made it easier for many respectable Chinese officials to parrot the official line in apparently sincere fashion, when they themselves do not believe a word of it. This was particularly the case in the hard-line Maoist period, but the official line will often still be delivered as gospel.

Another reason for the Chinese to dissemble is to save either you or them face; a lie is generally felt to be more acceptable than causing someone to lose face. They often try to avoid telling you what they think you would not want to hear, and some take this further and tell you what they think you do wish to hear, even if it is false. Simple good manners may also require a person to say what is proper for the occasion, rather than what is correct, and as with some Western sales personnel, a positive statement is often preferred to the truth.

If the blame for something not happening is placed upon another unit, the story might be true, but so much cooperation between units breaks down that it is a commonly used lie in order to conceal inefficiency, or even when the real reason is actually unknown. This is in sharp contrast to Japanese practice, where blaming another is frowned upon. Of course, like most people, the Chinese do not like to admit that they are wrong and some will continue to hide mistakes, even if it means lying to do so.

16 Do expect the Chinese to press for much free information. The Chinese frequently do not appreciate the costs of developing technology and might ask for, or even insist upon, a lot of free information, free training seminars and the like. Old friends and business partners are supposed to be supportive and some Chinese are genuinely bewildered to hear 'no'. Others have learned that real costs are involved, but still ask anyway. They

will use your hopes for future business to extract free consul-
tancy services from you. Proprietary rights are not always
respected and there is a widespread view that knowledge should
be shared. It is not unknown for China to import an item, then
reverse-engineer and copy it. Even samples supplied from abroad
hoping for sales have been used in this way. Many bookshops in
China have a special room, closed to foreigners, where pirated
copies of foreign books are on sale at low prices to locals.

17 Do expect to meet rather insensitive Chinese behaviour on
occasion. Some Chinese have an immense capacity for single-
minded behaviour. They will press and continue to press for
something and seemingly not get embarrassed or bored. They
will return to a subject previously decided and start again. This
self-centredness can surprise, and some Chinese can be very
insensitive to the feelings of foreigners. To such people, your
'face' is of no importance, only achieving what they wish. If you
have been asked to do something and do not want to, you can
try saying you will think about it and let them know. If you do
not get back to them on it, this means 'no'. This is a common
Chinese method. Should you find that the subject still keeps
being raised, you might have to make a polite but firm rejection.
Even a display of irritation and a threat to go over their head to
their boss might be needed. Most officials live in fear of
complaints and being investigated, as it allows their enemies in
the bureaucracy an opening to get them, so this gentle threat
should tame them. It is only to be used as a last resort, however,
as after such a threat they will probably not help you much in
the future and might actively hinder.

Contracts

18 Note that the attitude towards contracts is different and do not
be surprised if you are asked to change a contract. Differences
exist between foreigners and the Chinese about contract negotiation, approval, implementation and enforcement. During *negotiation,* the Chinese will often try to keep conditions vague where
the foreign side can benefit, but precise where Chinese interests
are at stake. If they are successful here, the foreigners' future
position is weakened. Generally, the Chinese feel they are
working towards a long-term relationship, the foreigners feel that
they are working towards signing a contract. Despite this general

attitude, you should try to get detailed clauses in the contract, even if the Chinese do not want them, and persist in this endeavour. Contracts have to be followed scrupulously and the Chinese tend to take the details very literally (even if demanding changes to agreed prices) so you should get in anything that you might need, even if this would be unusual in another country. You may have to fight to keep out anything you cannot abide. You should attempt to get a clause in the contract covering any adverse policy or price changes, although this may be resisted. Try to obtain a clause that says that both the English and Chinese versions are valid, as English can be a more precise language than Chinese. You can often put in addenda any minor details about the various responsibilities of each side.

During negotiations it is wise to keep notes of all items discussed and agreed and that will go in the contract later. Summing up what has been decided by reading them out at the end of each meeting is a good idea.

On the *approval* process, do not be shocked if after the contract is signed by all concerned some higher body, such as MOFERT (Ministry of Foreign Economic Relations and Trade) or the central bank, intervenes and demands renegotiations of points it does not like. Similarly, during negotiations, approval previously obtained from higher levels may suddenly be withdrawn.

With regard to *implementation*, contracts will be followed wherever possible but the attitude is not the same: the Chinese feel that contracts should be observed because of the status and respectability of the parties who signed to the agreed points, not because of the legal implications. It is sometimes difficult to implement a contract because of the sprawling bureaucracy and the difficulty of finding out who is responsible for causing a problem. New fees may be imposed, input prices suddenly increased, or instructions given to you to source purchases from a certain unit, which may not be the cheapest.

Expect that the Chinese side might ask for changes in a contract, even immediately after it is signed. The Chinese see nothing wrong with asking for a few changes. They do this for several reasons. One is that contracts are regarded differently in China from the West. They are considered not so much a legal document as an expression of good intent of the partners to the agreement. In addition, they know that foreigners place great store on the contract and the Chinese might want to change it to fit altered circumstances. Another possibility is that a new government policy may have been announced and the old contract does not quite accord. Some feel that the Chinese appear to believe in a theory of continual negotiations!

The general Chinese attitude, of course, allows you to ask for amendments to be made to the contract. With a Western background, you might not think of doing so. If you decide to, you might find that appeals to the earlier agreed general principles to show why the contract cannot be followed will be easily understood by the Chinese. They will understand and sympathize, even if they are forced to object to the change for business reasons.

The Chinese view that contracts can be renegotiated has led to dismay in the past. When the Chinese unilaterally cancelled some contracts at the end of the 1970s, they were surprised at the antagonistic attitude of the foreign partners. When in 1993 they refused to pay the contracted price for Australian wool, there was consternation in the Australian firms. The Chinese have also been known on occasion to offer to sign a contract that they have not yet seen, knowing that they can change it later. They have also sometimes terminated a contract early, on the basis that they feel that a signed contract means that both parties have a mutual interest and can work together to decide what is in the best interest of both.

The *enforcement* of contracts can be difficult. The legal situation is often difficult to deal with. In the eyes of the people, the law has never been all that important in China (see Note 21 below). When disputes arose between the parties that could not be settled, they were usually sent to arbitration by a third party acceptable to both, rather than to the courts. During negotiations, you might find that the Chinese object to binding arbitration clauses, just as you might fear that your rights are not fully protected without one.

Generally, you should always try to run the business without appealing to the contract, and build up a set of personal relationships as the core of doing business.

19 Do be careful with joint venture contract negotiations. With regard to joint ventures, you must expect that during the negotiations, the Chinese will try to give a high financial value to the land component that they supply as a major part of their share of the joint venture. You should ensure that furniture goes in the contract, and the provision of telephones, water and electricity can also be included with advantage. You definitely need a clause that covers the remittance of foreign exchange from your profits, which some have found difficult to do, despite it being legally allowed. Such a clause could usefully appear in non-joint venture sales' contracts too. Because materials and parts are often of low quality in China, it is helpful if you can get a clause that is vague on sources of supply, or allows foreign purchase without penalty if domestic quality is deficient, or local supplies are not available at a competitive price.

20 When in a joint venture, be prepared to face continuous renegotiations and suggested amendments of the contracts. If you try to enforce a contract by appealing to it, the Chinese partner might think you are merely an ignorant foreigner who does not realize that the words mean little. At the worst, he might even feel that you are trying to break the relationship and are telling him this in a subtle and indirect way. If a partner in a joint venture has to appeal to the signed contract, it is often a sign of a serious problem existing. The situation is not unlike a marriage if divorce is being considered and a prenuptial agreement is examined.

21 Note the different attitude to law and the preference for conciliation. The attitude to law is unlike that in the West. Historically, the Chinese have avoided recourse to the law courts. A popular saying was 'Go to the law, go to the devil'. The courts were part of the magistrate system which governed the huge population for the emperor in a massive country with poor communications. A major function was to keep the peace and prevent rebellion, which often meant holding down those who might prefer to rule themselves. The law courts were often concerned with these greater issues, rather than simply trying a case in an objective manner. In court a person could be treated harshly and even tortured to get at the truth, so there was good reason for this anti-law attitude. In addition, there might well be an unofficial presumption of guilt unless proved innocent, on the grounds that the person would not have been arrested unless they were bad.

Another reason for the different attitude towards the law is that Chinese society was based on a Confucian system of ethics, in which group relationship and proper behaviour mattered the most; the law became involved only when the proper Confucian relationships had broken down. The law was thus invoked only when the situation was already bad and someone must be guilty of something. Such attitudes persist to this day; ethics and moral principles are more important than law, and disputes tend to be handled at first through 'friendly consultation', and then by arbitration by a third party. Conciliation is preferred to arbitration. Litigation is strongly disliked. Even lawyers are regarded with suspicion and are often critically viewed as people who make a living by defending criminals and the guilty.

The Chinese have a deep sense of what is correct conduct and doing what is right. They have little sympathy for rebellious individuals acting against the group and breaking conformity.

Chinese laws and the legal system are in the process of being reformed and indeed parts are being newly established. During the Maoist period, the law was often put in abeyance, and it was broken with impunity by many official organizations and groups. During the left-wing periods, a newspaper editorial often had more strength than a law. This situation began to change after the introduction of reformist policies in December 1978, and many new laws and statutes have been drafted; lawyers trained; and the status of the legal system and profession raised. It is still the case, however, that many laws are rather vague and there are gaps in the legal coverage. There is now increased protection for trademarks, patents and copyright, especially with the new patent law of 1 January 1993, but in practice the law is often flouted. In addition to the national level, many laws and regulations have been promulgated locally, and they are often broad, vague or ambiguous, while some are not even internally consistent and others are mutually contradictory. It is fair to say that the law is still regarded in traditional fashion by many, i.e. something to be avoided and not of overriding importance.

22 Do note that internal and secret regulations exist that cannot be revealed to outsiders but which, in ignorance, it is easy to break. Despite their traditionally antagonistic attitude towards law, the Chinese will still quote it at you for their own purpose, and during negotiations they might tell you that secret regulations prevent something you want from being done. Even if not always true, there is little one can do about it. It is also irritating to be informed that you have transgressed secret regulations that you did not know existed and which will often still not be shown to you.

23 Note that politics are still regarded as being of prime importance in China. A sudden political change may be used to circumnavigate the law without warning.

24 Do observe that the Chinese often expect a 'sweetener' to be thrown into a deal near the end of negotiations. As negotiators,

the Chinese will often suddenly speed up as the time for signing the contract approaches, and start to focus on details and the actual words to be expressed in the contract. At this stage they might expect you to make a concession or two, almost as a quid pro quo for them agreeing to sign. Be prepared for this and make sure that you have kept something up your sleeve to give up – perhaps a price concession, a few free seminars, or a training trip abroad for one or two of their people. If selling on credit, it might be the time to announce a lower interest rate loan, which the Chinese often find more alluring than a cheaper price, or even some sort of major gift to the organization in order to celebrate the signing, such as a powerful refrigerator, computer, TV or hi-fi set.

6 Socializing and proper behaviour

1 You should be aware of the importance of banquets, which are held early in the evening. Banquets play a unique part in doing business with China. They serve to introduce new people, to reinforce existing relationships and to celebrate the conclusion of a deal. China is a poor country and low salaries for powerful people are common, so that free banquets can be considered to be an important part of their salary package. When you get to China, a banquet will be organized by your host unit. The more importance the Chinese place on your business/project, the more important will be the senior host. The Chinese present, who will be from various different units, will take note of the host's status and evaluate you accordingly. Banquets have a hidden agenda of making you feel warm and welcome as well as putting you under some obligation. You wipe the obligation slate clean by giving a reciprocal banquet for your host-unit after a decent interval, which might be a few days or a week. Good manners require you to do this in any case.

The Chinese eat early and a banquet often starts between 6 and 7 pm and lasts until around 8.30. It is usually held at a popular local restaurant and only rarely will you be invited to a Chinese home. It is felt that more face is gained for you by eating in a restaurant where the food is good, and in any case many Chinese homes are spartan and poor. A whole fish or perhaps fried rice will often be served towards the end of the meal. You will know when the meal is finally over, as a bowl or basket of fruit will be put on the table and cold (or hot) towels will usually be given for you to wipe your hands and face. After the towels, wait ten minutes and you have finished. In China, it is the function of the guest to initiate leaving, but some Chinese hosts now rise and say it was nice of you to come, etc., indicating that the evening is over.

The Chinese dress informally by Western standards, but, especially among the young, a degree of smartness is becoming desirable. For a banquet you should wear a suit and tie, as the Chinese are aware that this is smart wear for foreigners, even if they do not always subscribe themselves. There may also be other foreigners present who might look askance at you if you dress in casual garb. You will never need evening dress. If you are a woman, trouser suits are quite acceptable, as is a jumper and skirt, but you should be careful not to wear anything revealing, sexy or ostentatious, such as furs or a lot of jewellery.

2   Do observe the strict rules of greeting and seating. The host should greet the invited people and indicate where they should sit. It is polite to suggest that the main guest sits first, and the older people next, with the normal Confucian reverence for age. The leader (you) will be placed on the immediate right of the principal Chinese host. The 'best' seat is the one facing the door and with your back to the wall, and you and the main host will probably sit in that position.

Banquets follow a fairly set format in China. After seating, there will usually be light conversation, perhaps the cracking and eating of melon seeds, etc. and some cold hors d'oeuvres. When the principal host picks up his or her chopsticks it is the signal to start. Grace is never said. During the meal you should wait for the principal host to start on a dish before you sample it. Traditionally, the host has the duty of serving both food and wine to guests, but these days the wine is usually delegated to the waiters. The host will break into dishes like whole fish, using a fork and spoon or a set of serving-chopsticks, and serve the nearby (hence important) people. If using his own chopsticks, he will reverse them and use the blunt end that has not been near his mouth. If he serves you in this way, you should offer to do the same for him (and use the serving spoon or reverse your chopsticks) as this is polite. He might well decline – equally politely. You should learn to use chopsticks properly, but if you cannot manage at all, then quietly inform the host, or interpreter if language is a problem, and you will get Western eating implements.

Be particularly careful if business is raised not to make a promise to do something or agree to a clause that you might regret later. Stick to safe topics of conversation, unless the Chinese initiate something, and avoid the unsafe (see Chapter 1, Note 33).

Pace your eating, and try only a small bit of each dish, as there will be more courses than you probably imagine. The host will have a menu by his side – if you can count the written lines, you know the number of dishes to be served. Note that it would be rude to stop eating in the middle of the banquet, even if you are feeling bloated, as traditionally it is a silent criticism of the food, of something said, or perhaps of the Chinese side in general.

3   Do note the importance of toasting and its etiquette. Early in the proceedings, the host will rise and toast the main guest, and the delegation, and perhaps their country of origin. After a few minutes, often after the next course has been served, the main guest rises and responds, toasting in return. It is best to follow the line established, and toast to success and the business at hand, the friendship of your two nations, cooperation between the two companies, etc. You toast the Chinese team itself and if the host toasted your country you must do the same for theirs. Always refer to China as 'The People's Republic of China' and Taiwan as 'the Province of Taiwan', but do not refer to Taiwan as a country.

There will be several glasses on the table, one reserved for toasts, usually in a strong spirit such as *maotai*. Be on your guard, for individual members of the Chinese team might toast your health one after the other – they take one sip each, but with eight toasts you get eight mouthfuls and the spirit is strong. You are allowed to return toasts in lighter wine, beer, or even the ubiquitous orange juice, but *maotai* has a rather macho image for the Chinese. They might enquire how many glasses you are able to drink. Note that it is important not to start the evening on alcohol then switch to fruit juice, etc. as this might inadvertently pass the symbolic message that you have been annoyed or insulted. Traditionally, it is impolite to pour your own drink as it is the responsibility of the host to keep an eye on your glass and refill it. This view still lingers and the waiter should notice the empty glass. They usually do so with gusto and it is easy to drink more than one thinks, as they keep on filling up one's glass. If the Chinese host rises and walks around toasting people individually, when he gets to you, rise to your feet and reciprocate the toast.

4   Do note that table manners are different in China. The food is cut up in the kitchen, or in the case of a few soft dishes with a spoon and fork in front of you, so that everything can be eaten with chopsticks. This means that there is no need to touch the

food with your fingers and indeed that is very bad manners. The exception to this is with large steamed buns, large shellfish and sometimes with chicken or duck legs and wings. Wait and see if the host picks up with his fingers before you do. Your personal chopsticks should never be put in the communal bowl in these days of AIDS, so you use the spoon or special serving chopsticks provided. Reversing the chopsticks and using the blunt end in the communal dish is quite acceptable. Ideally, the end of the chopsticks should not actually be put in the mouth but merely to it and the food removed with the mouth, but few foreigners aspire to such niceties. If you are left-handed you have a problem, in that when you are eating your left elbow will probably knock into your neighbour's right elbow, so both your chopsticks can open and the food fall. Chinese parents force their left-handed children to eat with chopsticks in the right hand for this reason. If left-handed, you will just have to be aware and careful. If you do inadvertently send someone's food flying in this way, smile and apologize profusely for your clumsiness.

You do not have to eat everything provided, so that if you get some piece that you do not like, like a chicken's foot or head, just leave it. In cheap restaurants the unwanted bits of food, bones, gristle, etc. may be placed on the table by your plate, but in decent restaurants this is considered bad manners and any unwanted bits should be placed on the small plate provided under your personal bowl. This may be emptied by a waiter from time to time. It is regarded as bad manners to sift through the communal dish looking for a particularly nice morsel – you should first select by looking carefully and then pick up the chosen piece. It is not bad manners to pick up your personal bowl to eat from, and the Chinese think it strange that foreigners do not do this. They sometimes say things like 'one would think foreigners' bowls were glued to the table'. Waiters serve and clear from either side. Noisy eating is not regarded as bad manners, so that slurping tea and soup, or talking with the mouth full, is quite normal in China. Curiously enough, belching is not thought polite. You may put your elbows on the table with impunity, however, and, unlike English good manners, you may move your soup spoon towards you in the bowl when eating.

Most Chinese use toothpicks after a meal and this is a polite thing to do – if you follow suit, you must cover your mouth with the free hand and use it surreptitiously, as they do.

5   Do be prepared to discuss Chinese food. The Chinese love talking about food and comparing dishes, restaurants and the various provincial styles of Chinese cooking. The more Westernized and travelled may compare France with China and you might encounter a discussion on whether Marco Polo took noodles from China to Italy, where they are called spaghetti (they will probably insist he did!), or brought them to China in the first place.

6   Do be prepared to make a gracious speech or even sing. In the speech you should refer to matters such as the warm and continuing relationship between the two sides, the intention of both sides to do business, China's good economic progress, your hopes for China's future, the past and present friendship between your two nations, the mutual benefits of the project, future friendship and harmony between the two firms, and the like. Once the Chinese get to know you, you might also find that at more relaxed banquets, or at the farewell one, they produce a singer or two, often brought in for this purpose. If this happens, take it as an advance warning that they will shortly ask you to sing in return and probably insist on it. It is a good idea to practise something beforehand or at least to have worked out who in the team will sing what. A typical song or your own country, a folk song, or sea shanty is quite acceptable. Avoid anything from *The Sound of Music,* as too many foreigners have sung such selections for years, the Chinese are bored with it, and some are cautious about it because it was reputedly a favourite film of Chiang Ching, the politically disgraced wife of Mao Zedong. At the farewell banquet you should praise any agreements reached and if things went badly and no agreements were signed, you should at least refer to the fruitful talks and express hopes for the future. Avoid all jokes in speeches, speak slowly and finish quickly.

7   Remember to leave early after the meal finishes, although the Chinese will indicate that it is time, usually by some remark or by the leader shuffling and standing while smiling and thanking you, etc. Recall that the guest is the one who should make the move to depart.

8   Do note that you must give a return banquet if you went to one. Ask your Chinese contact person, the interpreter or host which is a good restaurant and ask the contact how best to organize it and how much per head would be about right. He or she will probably suggest that they themselves or the interpreter can do it. Choose the guest-list carefully and take advice from the contact person and interpreters about who should be there. Not inviting someone who should be there is an insult. The restaurant should be booked for the correct number, several days in advance. A private room will normally be used. Most restaurants will choose the menu for you, and often merely need to know how much per head you are prepared to spend.

As host, you must ensure that the guests are met at the door and escorted to the room where you welcome them. The seating must be strictly by protocol, principal guest on your right, and this is where your contact/Chinese interpreter can help decide. Recall that any lists of names the Chinese supplied earlier will be in protocol order, which helps a bit. Getting it wrong is an insult. Their group leader as the main guest is placed at the immediate right of the host; their deputy leader should sit on the right of your next highest person opposite if using a round table. If the numbers dictate two tables, your second-in-command should act as host on the second table, but the deputy Chinese leader should sit at the first table together with all the senior guests. If you must use a long table, your second-in-command sits at the far end with the deputy Chinese leader on his or her right. One interpreter should be on the immediate right of the Chinese leader and one on the right of his deputy. The hosts and guests sit alternately but some might have relatively little English, although they often speak and understand more than at first appears.

Place-cards with names, in the two languages, are used, and you should show each person where they are to sit.

At the close of the evening you should escort them to the door. If there are many of them, you and your team can stand at the door in pecking-order line and make your farewells.

You settle the bill after all the guests have departed, never in their presence. Note that there is no concept of sharing the bill even in ordinary restaurants, for there is always a host and the guests, and if it is not a formal banquet, the Chinese will usually fight to pay and be the host, which gains face.

7 How to treat visitors to one's own country

1   Do expect to have to organize Chinese visitors thoroughly, much
more than for most foreign guests. In China in their ordinary
existence everything is arranged for them, as it was for you when
you were there. They are simply unused to the freedom of deciding for themselves where to stay, where to eat and what to visit.
Really Westernized and well-travelled Chinese can cope with it,
but would probably still feel insulted that you had not bothered.
It means a lot of work for your PA or secretary and you must
keep an eye on it to ensure that what is organized is appropriate. It is not only hotel bookings and travel that must be
organized in advance, you should also allocate a contact person
for them. He or she should accompany them, pick them up at
the hotel, bring them to your office, take them to lunch or out
in the evening etc., much as in China. A Chinese speaker is useful
for this. If this person has to leave them for reasons of business,
he or she can suggest 'Perhaps you would like to rest for the
remainder of the afternoon' which will be understood. Often they
like the idea of just relaxing after a strenuous visit.

2   Do ensure that your Chinese visitors are met at the airport,
which is a basic courtesy of the Chinese. If possible, do this
yourself, as this gives them face. If you have a tame corporation
president whose function it is to do such things, this would be
even better, but if you both go that would be best. If you produce
a high-ranking figure from your firm, it shows how seriously you
are taking the visit and gives much face. Remember that China
is hierarchical and leader greets leader first, before moving on to
second-stringers. Interpreters rank last. It is essential that you
remind yourself of the names before they arrive (business cards
that you previously annotated and/or a photograph may help you
here) and it is desirable that you have learned the names of any
new members before the delegation arrives.

You must also escort them to the airport when they depart, or arrange for them to be taken. You should accompany them as far as is possible, not leave them in the concourse or bar, etc. The Chinese know things are done differently abroad and will make allowances, but it is human nature to be easily flattered or insulted. For diplomatic travel they should always be met and escorted, for private business it is merely an extremely good idea.

3   You should let the Chinese live together if they are staying some time in your city. For short visits of a few days a good hotel is now desirable. Only a few years ago it could have been of moderate or even low standard, unless the visitor was around ministerial rank or you were really trying to impress. Those Chinese who have travelled abroad a few times have now become accustomed to top hotels and these days may feel insulted if put in a cheaper one.

If, however, the Chinese are staying longer than a few days, perhaps for a month or so for training, you should let them share and live together in a fairly cheap place. It may seem spartan accommodation to you, but they will be more used to this and less bewildered by the change of scene. Expect them to live cheaply and economize. They will be unused to your high prices and will prefer to save money where they can, cooking for themselves in what might seem slightly shabby surroundings to you. They would probably be horrified if you were to supply a cleaning and cooking service, and may seriously question the way you waste money and start to wonder whether you might in fact be an unsuitable person with whom to do business. Similarly, an expensive long-term stay in a modern hotel might worry them and could even cause them, for example, to consider backing out of a proposed joint venture.

For such longer stayers a few simple rules help. Few Chinese can drive a motorcar so that easy access to safe public transport is a must. If the traffic in your town permits, and they are technicians, etc. who are there for training rather than high-level company presidents, you might suggest buying them a bicycle each. This might be much appreciated, as it is the normal form of transport for most people in China. You are unlikely to have to host a really senior Chinese for an extended period, for whom a motorcar and driver might be necessary.

In the evening the delegation will be happy to stay together and watch TV, talk, fill in their detailed daily diary and amuse themselves. Even a weekend can be passed this way, although an organized and accompanied trip out would be appreciated. Often a few books in Chinese, available cheaply in Hong Kong (such as detective stories), are enjoyed and you could leave a few in the hotel room or apartment for their use. You should get a local Chinese to glance over them and ensure that they are not pornographic or insulting about China, etc., which would be embarrassing. The Chinese often enjoy such lightweight, rather trashy novels, as they are rare or sometimes even banned in China.

4   You should entertain them in a good Chinese restaurant. The Chinese prefer their own food and have difficulty facing large slabs of meat, which after a lifetime of only seeing small pieces they often find quite repulsive. Many Chinese also tend to eat a lot of vegetables rather than meat, a product of necessity in a poor country. They rarely enjoy dairy products, including cheese, which often gives them indigestion. A good Chinese restaurant that specializes in seafood is always a safe bet.

If it is a formal banquet recall the seating arrangements (see Chapter 6, Notes 2 and 8) and observe the customary Chinese etiquette if you can.

5   Although taking them to a good Chinese restaurant honours the visitors, if you have met them before they will probably be pleased and interested to visit your home to see what it is like. They will undoubtedly find it extraordinarily palatial and well furnished, and are likely to ask if such a big home is typical of how people live in your country.

8 *Living in China*

1   Do note that it is hard to choose a joint venture partner. There are many potential firms and you should be cautious. Approaching CCPIT and your embassy is a good first step, but you should talk to other business people and keep your ears open. Firms are organized on geographical or functional lines. Major decisions which need a lot of thought include whether to choose a national, provincial or city-level firm, and where to locate e.g. in a Special Economic Zone; in Shanghai; or in the booming southern delta area around Guangzhou, etc.

2   Accept that you need to base a male expat in China to manage the firm if you open a joint venture. The level of Chinese management is not high and one of the reasons they want joint ventures is to gain modern management training and techniques. You will not be able to rely solely on Chinese management, nor would you wish to do so, if you are putting up the money and skills. The need for an expat may be less pronounced if the joint venture is in simple primary produce with little processing involved.

It is better to send a man to live and work in China. As in most countries, the Chinese are essentially male chauvinistic by tradition and although the Communist Party and the government have made strong efforts to alter this, including putting equal rights into the Constitution, the legal situation does not exactly coincide with reality. In rural China, women are not regarded as equals nor treated equally; in urban China the attitude towards women depends in large part upon the level of education – the more educated males are more likely to be tolerant and egalitarian. Those who work in state-run enterprises may also be more tolerant, partly the result of 'education' sessions they have been forced to attend and partly because they see personal benefits from having two incomes in the family. The inequality situation has improved but is still not perfect. In general, however, the Chinese are less worried about a manager being female, especially among foreigners, than are the Japanese. A married partner should accompany the person to China if possible to make it easier to cope with the life there.

3   Do select a suitable person. The man will be chosen for professional and technical expertise and will have to do a lot of coping with the unexpected and making fast decisions, which means a detailed knowledge of the product and process. In addition, consideration must be given to trying to find someone who is mature, flexible and likely to fit into the local situation with understanding. Patience and gentle stubbornness are desirable too. Someone with previous overseas experience, and that in Asia for preference, would be best. Experience of poverty or living in poor circumstances would probably be an advantage. Former military people or those who have survived a boarding school might have an advantage, in that they have been trained to endure privation and perhaps intense periods of work followed by stretches of boredom.

The wife should also be considered when the decision on which man to send is made. Unless there is clearly only one person in the firm who could go, which is not likely unless the firm is small, then the spouse should also be flexible, open-minded, tolerant, able to adjust, etc. As loneliness is likely to be a problem for the spouse, someone who is self-reliant is preferable. If the spouse is unhappy, the manager will probably be miserable. If the marriage is going through a bad patch, it would be unwise to send them. The China experience could cause a rallying round and solidify the relationship, but it is far more likely to aggravate tensions and lead to breakdowns of marriage and, possibly, people. For many people there is an immense stress from merely living in China.

If the children are experiencing difficulties at home or could in any sense be considered to be 'problem children' they should not be sent. It would be preferable to send a different family than increase the danger of premature withdrawal of the manager for family reasons.

4   Do ensure that suitable pre-departure training is done in order to minimize culture shock. At least three months before departure, the family as well as the manager should be involved in a familiarization and training programme, in order to minimize culture shock and unhappiness. Anyone going to live and work in China can expect to suffer from culture shock. Extended

training is desirable, despite what may seem to be a high cost involved – pre-departure training actually saves money if the firm does not have to recall an expat early because of problems.

Training might take several forms:

- Carefully selected brochures and hand-outs about the country, its history, culture, standard of living and ways of life. Photographs might be helpful here.
- Videos and films about the country to be borrowed by the company and loaned to the family. This could usefully include films made in China that may reveal attitudes and more of the culture.
- Discussions with anyone in the company who has visited and, in particular, previously lived in China. This might best be done over a dinner in a private home, when people are relaxed and might speak more freely.
- Enrolling the wife as well as the manager in any locally available night-classes or day-courses on China, at company expense.

5   What to warn a family about. Reading this book is a start. It is impossible to cover everything that might be encountered in any country and there is no good substitute for experience. China is quite different from most countries, even other Asian ones. There is much that will delight and fascinate, but there is more that will surprise, and might even shock. China is a poor country, and poor to a degree that can startle. In China, people who share kitchens or bathrooms with other families are not regarded as poor but as quite well off; after all, they must have living accommodation of their own to be able to share such facilities.

In recent years, prices have risen substantially after decades of being fixed; acceptable political and social attitudes have changed significantly in the past decade or so; foreigners are now much in evidence; the people and children are not constantly told (and shown films and contemporary newsreels) that the Japanese are 'poisonous dwarves' who raped Nanking and bayoneted babies. The extent and rapidity of change is considerable and stress levels are high.

Dealing with the bureaucracy can be an infuriating part of being in China. Even ordinary matters like organizing a trip can be time-consuming and frustrating at the least; at the worst, after a request has been tabled, no reply might ever be received. Just getting permits to do something can take up days of effort.

With regard to ordinary living matters, the availability of goods and services taken for granted in the West cannot be assumed. This can be a constant source of aggravation. Service in restaurants and hotels in particular has been awful for decades and despite recent improvement, China is often well behind international standards, although some of the modern hotels do well.

It is important to buy a good bicycle. Chinese bicycles are poor – typically as delivered from the best factories the spokes are so slack that the wheels will not turn, and the buyer is forced to wheel or perhaps carry it straight to a small local private shop where it is entirely dismantled and rebuilt. Such 'repair shops' exist everywhere in cities – they also mend punctures, etc. It is important to get it rebuilt before you try to ride it.

Accommodation can prove to be difficult. It is probable that no house will be available for rent and the family will be forced to spend the whole period in China living in a hotel. Some people find this claustrophobic and, without a home of their own, feel unhappy. If one is lucky enough to get a house, it will probably be in a small foreign ghetto located in an area that is inconvenient for shopping, the city centre, or where the manager works. Because of the shortage of office space, he may well be working out of a hotel, as well as living in one.

Shopping is not particularly enjoyable. There are not many supermarkets in the Western sense, with goods piled high, and a high range and a variety of produce and prices. Those supermarkets recently established with foreign assistance are quite good, but the local ones are often not the equivalent of those in the West. Chinese supermarkets tend to resemble old-fashioned Western department stores, with goods displayed under glass. The range of goods is small and until recently much that was on display was not actually available for sale, so that it was more like an industrial display than a shop. There are still few high-quality stores. Antique shops exist but are often run by the state, are very expensive and nothing more than about 150 years old can be taken out of the country without special permission. Clothing and shoe sizes are difficult, as Chinese are, on average, smaller than occidentals and not many large sizes are available. What is available is frequently of poor design, often ugly and tends to fall apart quickly. The situation has improved in recent years, but it is still below Western standards.

The brand names with which Westerners are familiar are usually absent; if present they have normally been made in

China, which in some cases mean lower quality, if the item was intended for export but rejected because of inadequate quality. Things such as cheese are not readily available, nor is milk outside the major cities. Fruit and meat are now more plentiful, thanks to free markets, but the price can be high.

Health can be a problem. China is a country in which it is easy to get sick – almost all visiting Westerners go down with upper respiratory tract infections, colds, tonsilitis, etc. This is worse in the north and west, due to the dust-storms blowing in from the desert. It is essential to take plenty of medicines, especially if you have children, to cover all normal 'visit the doctor' situations in a Western country. If in Beijing, the embassy doctor can sometimes be persuaded to take one on. Serious illness can be a problem – if it looks serious or could develop serious complications, it is important to fly to Tokyo or Hong Kong at once.

Dental care is not generally good and teeth should be fixed before departure. Even Beijing is poor in this regard and the Central Committee members are popularly believed to fly to Chengdu in south-west China for their dental treatment as there is a good dental hospital there. Spectacles, on the other hand, are cheap, generally available, and I have not heard their quality criticized.

Boredom and feelings of isolation are common problems for spouses – there is nowhere much to go, while travel is uncomfortable and may be restricted by the authorities to a few miles locally. There is no cinema with films in English, nor any theatre except for the traditional Chinese type, which is best described as an acquired taste for a small minority. There are no swimming pools or country clubs, and few bars in which one can meet people except in top hotels. Once one has seen the local temples, the Great Wall and so on, there is not a lot to do.

Children face special difficulties. They will have only a small peer group speaking English – probably none if outside a major city. The family's children will have to learn Chinese to communicate. The Chinese want to practise English with foreigners, indeed it can be a nuisance being buttonholed in hotel lobbies. The education of the children is a real issue. Depending on age, it might be better for their education to leave them in their own country in a boarding school, as colonial people often did in the past. However, if this course is adopted then the parents will miss them and be even more bored. If the non-working spouse is a teacher he or she could perhaps set up a local English school for any other expats. This would help them to solidify their place in the social group and give the children playmates.

The family would be well advised to take lots of novels, books, cassettes, videos of films, etc., and the equipment to play them on. A good short-wave radio is an asset and allows you to stay in touch with the outside world. Perhaps one or two computers and lots of games would be a help – more than one person may wish to use the computer at the same time. Recall that the electric voltage tends to vary a lot without warning and this can destroy really sophisticated hi-tech equipment, so it needs to be sturdy as well as good. A laptop and lots of batteries might be an advantage. It would be beneficial to have a friend, perhaps in the company, regularly send out things like new videos, as well as CDs, books, magazines, and the latest computer games.

It might be helpful if the family sent their address in China to all their friends and relatives a month before they leave and not wait until they arrive. Mail can take two weeks or more to get through and a strong feeling of isolation and being cut off from the real world can easily develop in the first month's wait to receive a letter. Regular correspondence is a valuable commodity; it provides a great outlet for emotions and for feeling wanted. It would be possible to make a small rubber stamp of the address in Chinese or, alternatively, print up hundreds of sticky labels for the grandparents or other close relatives to stick on the envelope. This speeds up the delivery in China, sometimes considerably, as letters tend to be held up in the post office waiting for perhaps the only person who can read English to get over an illness and return to work.

When in China one should not be surprised to see adult males walking along holding hands; this shows close friendship and has no sexual connotation. In Westernized Hong Kong, on the other hand, it would have a clear homosexual feel about it.

One must expect to be stared at as an unusual object and one should try not to become annoyed. It is common to be pointed out to children, or to other adults in a group who may not have noticed the presence of such a strange being. This is not considered rude in China. The more remote the district, the more likely it is to happen, but even in cosmopolitan Shanghai when away from the main tourist area I was once followed for a kilometre or more by a crowd of perhaps 200 people.

Given the difficulties of living and working in China, the company should have a fallback position in case major problems occur. It should be prepared to move the wife and children to Hong Kong if things get desperate and the manager be allowed to visit, say, every two or three weeks. Alternatively, the wife and children might prefer to return home and visit the manager in China, say, annually.

Establish the ground rules before departure

6   Make clear the company expectations of the manager's role. The company must decide in advance what the manager is expected to do or achieve. 'To run the branch properly' is not enough. Is he, for example, expected to raise profits, sales, total revenue or market share, and if so, by how much? Or is it envisaged that new product lines should be developed? These expectations should be discussed and clearly understood on both sides. This way, some idea of what constitutes success or failure will be apparent, and the manager will be more certain about the priorities to be attached to different duties.

7   All must agree on the need to communicate with headquarters. The manager and his spouse should be aware of what is desired; for instance, a monthly or quarterly report sent either by post or fax; or perhaps a fortnightly telephone call to a specified person in headquarters both to maintain contact and dispel any feelings of isolation. It should be made clear that the manager must send a fax or make a telephone call at any time if a really urgent matter arises that should have headquarters approval or awareness (e.g. rioting workers that could turn into an international incident).

8   Everyone should be aware of the manager's career path and reassurance should be offered about his position in the firm. One problem that expats often face is a fear of being forgotten, overlooked in promotion considerations, losing out to rivals at headquarters, and even a worry that the overseas assignment may count against rather than for them, upon their return. The manager will function better if he knows that such fears are common among expats and in his case are groundless. He could try to find a mentor or guide to look after his interests in the headquarters of the firm while he is abroad; although this is perhaps not common in Western culture, it is quite usual in Asian ones and serves a useful purpose.

9   Training after arrival is required. It takes time to settle in, feel reasonably at home, and begin to function efficiently. Local orientation is essential. If replacing someone, an easy and valuable way is to allow an overlap, say of one or two weeks, between the change-over of managers. For business efficiency, this allows the new manager to get into the job, see how it is done, and note any differences from the methods that are used at home and find out why this is sensible in China. It also allows him to meet the right people, such as the powerful local officials, local business people, and other expats. It is particularly important for the incoming person to be introduced by the outgoing manager, and not merely to take over the branch and introduce himself. Trust in China comes from being introduced, not automatically from the position occupied. Respect, on the other hand, can come with the position, and often does not have to be earned, unlike in most Western countries.

A more formal way would be to set up training and orientation sessions, preferably for manager and spouse together, with lectures, films, slides, videos, etc. about what to expect now they have arrived, how to behave, what to do about common problems that will be encountered, etc. If the existing manager or company has put together any pamphlets, brochures or hint-sheets, these should be distributed and studied. It would be a useful task for the spouse to compile such a compendium if one does not exist, which would be valuable for future people as well as giving her an interest and purpose in life.

After a few days to get over jet-lag, a large reception could usefully be hosted by the company, to introduce the new couple to both expats and Chinese, and this would be appreciated as a polite and enjoyable way of making introductions. Chinese are not comfortable trying to eat standing up and balancing drinks and plates, nor do most of them tend to drink a lot. A sit-down dinner is therefore generally preferable to a buffet-style one or a drinks-only party.

10   Do expect that headquarters will start to worry about whose side the expat is on. Once the manager understands the job and business culture well enough to function properly in China, the staff back at headquarters will probably start wondering if he has 'gone native' and begun to consider the interests of the Chinese more than those of the firm. The gradual assimilation into Chinese ways, which is needed in order to be more effective for the firm, often means a cross-cultural clash between the expat and the headquarters staff. For his part, the expat will probably feel that headquarters does not understand either him or the difficult situation on the ground. If both the manager and headquarters staff expect this, then it can perhaps more easily be tackled.

11 Coping with the realities of China. China is a poor country, lacks a good basic infrastructure, and many of the things usually taken for granted can be of low quality, function badly or be totally absent. There are far more things that can surprise and shock than can be mentioned and it is impossible to know what will startle a particular person. Such things as a lack of drinking water from taps so that all water must be boiled, the unavailability of known brand-named goods, outside major cities the limited range of food and fruit in the market, or the TV that cannot be understood, upset some. The lack of familiar music on the radio that can be enjoyed, the noisy throat clearing and spitting that will be encountered, or the sight of men pulling small carts loaded with human manure, or occasional women pulling handcarts loaded with heavy goods, can upset others. The water supply can still go off without warning and in a large block or hotel, the higher the floor you are on, the more likely it is that the water will go off.

Letting off steam is important as a safety-valve but often this is not easy to do. Loud swearing or shouting in a soundproof room, or beating stuffed images with wooden sticks might prove to be ideal for many, but such practices do not seem to be common or acceptable outside a few Japanese companies. Frustration will be felt, and some way of alleviating it must be found. Some have found that taking a 'treasure box' containing personally selected reminders of home that each family member packs before leaving helps. Perhaps watching videos about your own country or well-known films or a TV series would help. There are two different approaches involved: (1) relieve the frustration in some active way; or (2) remove oneself temporarily from reality and live in a sort of dream-world, a pretended return to one's own world. The latter may be psychologically less useful, or even damaging, as it ducks reality rather than faces it. But whatever proves to help the individual is probably valuable and worth doing.

9 Managing joint ventures

1   When you have set up a joint venture using a go-between or help-mate, do keep him in the area long enough to make friends and teach you how best to operate. He should introduce you around and help you settle in.

2   With regard to joint venture organization, you should try to get control of more than half the management board. This will make future problem solving easier. If yours is a new factory, when it is ready to start operating, do examine the production processes carefully to see if they are complete. The Chinese have been known to replace a section of the foreign-designed production line by more labour-intensive methods to try to boost employment. If they have done so, put things back or risk facing reduced productivity and perhaps quality. If you have a 100 per cent foreign ownership firm, you might find it beneficial to hire a local cadre to act as a buffer between you and the workers, rather like the old comprador system of pre-1949. Even Taiwanese firms in China tend to do this, as the locals understand the system better and it seems to work well.

3   Materials and supplies in China can be of low or variable quality and it is hoped that you have obtained a contract which allows for choice of source. If not, you might find problems of quality control causing the product not to be exportable. A complex distribution system involving poor transport and warehousing faces you, and deliveries often arrive late. It is wise to bring with you your own office equipment, such as computer, copier, tape recorder and typewriter. These used to be almost impossible to get in China, and although the situation improves steadily, if you know you have your equipment it is one less thing to worry about. If a reliable electricity supply is necessary, you should take your own generator and make sure that you have spare parts for it.

4   Do be careful about initiating changes. The Chinese system is quite different from the Western ones you are accustomed to, and what works in London, New York or Sydney may fail in China. If the Chinese do a thing in a way different from yours, it may still be the most sensible way to operate. You might find your suggestions politely received and then ignored. Sometimes a refusal to do what you want is merely innate conservatism and rejection of a foreign idea, or a failure to appreciate why you want it done that way and what benefits will ensue. At other times you will be ignored because your way would simply not work well. Listen carefully to suggestions the Chinese may make, there is often a good reason for them even if it is not immediately obvious to you. Ask your go-between, especially if he is Chinese, why they might want it done that way.

5   Do try not to admit to problems to the Chinese, even of managerial level, but quietly set about solving them. Culturally, the Chinese tend to see a person with obvious problems as an incompetent, rather than someone facing up to and tackling a challenge. If you must explain some change that you will make, do it in detail and then relate it to the big picture, so that the interlinked process and system can be seen. For the Chinese, cause and effect often matter less than being able to appreciate the interrelationships.

6   Do expect large numbers of people to be squashed into rooms, either to work or to attend briefings or training sessions. China is a poor country with a huge population, and space is at a premium. People are used to living and working in conditions that might appal you. Other poor conditions you might encounter include homes and offices that are extremely hot in summer and freezing cold in winter, factories with no safety equipment on high-speed cutting machines, and workshops with slippery, greasy floors.

7   Do expect that product style and fashion will loom low in Chinese eyes and much time must be spent promoting the idea that such things matter. Although the Chinese have a history of appreciating beauty and culture, the Manchu dynasty (1644–1911) had rather poor taste that favoured the garish and obvious. More recently, the central planning system, with its ethos of scarcity and seller's market, also strongly discouraged an interest in quality and design. Even the political partnership and cult of personality under Chairman Mao was unhelpful, in that it caused the widespread distribution of millions of ugly political artefacts.

You must keep an eye on production and if you supply special buttons, etc. to improve product design, you might discover that the workers may not bother to use them. You must spend time both showing what you want and explaining why. There are now a relatively small number of Chinese, the rough equivalent of yuppies, who are tremendously interested in style. Things are improving, if slowly.

8   Do note that costs can be higher than expected and the infrastructure is weak. Because of poor quality of materials, you might have to import instead of being able to rely on local ones. It is not unusual to feel that one is constantly engaged in a battle with an invisible but all-powerful bureaucracy, along the lines of a novel by Franz Kafka. Machinery breaks down regularly for several reasons: maintenance is not taken seriously, skilled technicians and engineers are in short supply, spare parts are lacking, and power fluctuations take their toll, as do dust in the centre and north, or humidity in the south.

Workers' costs may not be as low as you would hope, because low productivity can offset a part of the low wage paid. The Chinese managers may ask for the same salary and package as the expats, despite lacking knowledge and experience, and in many cases are really high-level apprentices. They do this for reasons of face as well as wishing to increase their standard of living. Note that they may not actually receive the salary you pay them, as the government may take most of it as a sort of tax on you. If all the expats in the joint venture have a car, it may pay you to give each Chinese manager one as well, as a car is a symbol of power and a very scarce item. If the Chinese do not have one also, they will feel a loss of face and might become demoralized or actually obstructive.

Hidden costs abound and the Chinese may spring a range of costs on you even after the contract has been signed. Note that a feasibility study done for you may exclude some necessary costs, so it is wise to get worker services fully spelled out in writing. These may include training, housing subsidies, health care, a crèche or school, free lunches, and a variety of strange allowances (e.g. for haircuts). Land-use fees should also be spelled out, and any connection charges or establishment fees for public utilities, such as water, electricity, gas and telephones, clearly indicated. Chinese New Year may require a double monthly salary for all workers, or a present such as a basket of food. Expect that workers you have trained might suddenly be removed and new ones supplied, adding to costs. The slow pace of negotiations which involve you spending time in China add to the cost of the deal, especially for small firms. Banquets, 'study tours' and free trips for officials might not be listed on paper but you will probably end up paying for such items.

Some costs are high because of use of a multi-price system in China. Foreigners are aggrieved, often justifiably, about the habit of charging high prices for foreigners but low ones for the Chinese for things such as travel by aircraft or train, hotel rooms or meals. In addition, office and housing costs for foreigners are generally high by international standards.

Labour and incentives

9   Do observe the importance of hierarchy in the firm and treat the higher-level Chinese managers with respect. In practical terms, age matters, so try to promote people who are older and do not put someone very young over someone middle-aged or old. If you break this rule, neither person would be comfortable and the system would not work well. Promotion by merit is something of an alien concept in China, but if there is no alternative to putting a younger person over an older, you might get by if you pay the older the same (higher) salary as the younger. It would be particularly unfortunate to put a younger woman over an older man.

   Those in supervisory positions get perks such as trips, and you should watch to ensure that all get a turn and no one is left out while others go twice. If this should happen it can cause great resentment and loss of face; even those benefiting would think that you were not competent to understand China or run the firm properly. You must accept the slight loss of efficiency involved in sending someone who is not really the most suitable person for the task at hand.

10   Do expect Chinese managers to be reluctant to make decisions and sign documents. Patience and training is needed to allow Chinese managers to overcome fear, develop a feeling of responsibility and become willing to take decisions. If you go away from the joint venture on a trip, etc., you might find that few decisions will be made during your absence, however pressing the problem. With time, effort and patience, this can usually be overcome. Chinese managers are often reluctant to sign documents as in the past they could be punished severely or sent to work as labourers merely for signing something later judged to be politically incorrect.

When they do send documents, the message is often short and peremptory in style, resembling a curt order without any semblance of politeness. You should show them how to draft polite requests to help them to overcome their often abrupt style.

11 Do retain any existing perks for managers, such as banquets. The food eaten cannot be taxed, and face is gained by attending such events. Do observe that if you are having problems of delays with customs or other local officials, inviting them to a few dinners is often a good way of ensuring that the problems suddenly disappear. A quiet gift of a bottle of brandy or a carton of cigarettes may not come amiss here, but really major problems may require a bigger gift, such as a TV or refrigerator. This is a difficult area and it may depend on how far you are willing to go ethically in order to work more efficiently within the local system.

12 Do anticipate having to explain things in great detail. This is partly because although the Chinese love details, they also need to see how the picture fits together. They are unfamiliar with Western business practices, and they are often a little afraid and unsure what is required of them. You might find that your managers as well as your workers are rather literally minded and do not do something that obviously needs doing, simply because you did not ask them. If it is not clearly laid down in their job description or falls in their direct area it is often ignored. Rule following and obeying orders is far more prevalent than creativity, or lateral thinking. It is therefore essential to specify everything carefully.

13 Work incentives in most joint ventures take the form of wages higher than those paid in Chinese firms, together with a variety of bonuses. You should also post signs on walls to encourage workers, as they are used to and respond to such methods. A notice board with slogans at the entrance and on the front lawn can encourage people to work harder, raise quality or pursue whatever goal you nominate. Putting the name of the 'worker of the month' on the board or even individual photographs of successful workers can be used with some success, as the approach gives much 'face'. Methods such as these have been used for decades and if you do not do this, the workers might just think that you do not take production, service, quality, etc. seriously.

Workers usually lack experience and often have difficulty in accepting Western-style discipline and hard work. They tend to stop work perhaps ten minutes early in anticipation of a coffee break, and in state-run firms may have got used to sitting around reading newspapers, playing cards or even sleeping while at work. Note that some workers might have been released from their existing job because they were not good. Most state firms try to retain their better workers and may refuse to release them. Most joint ventures have found that it can take a couple of years before the workers are really working well, but the low wage rates do tend to compensate for the lower productivity.

14   Disciplining workers is not easy, as it may be difficult or even impossible to fire them. Even if successful here, the replacement workers will certainly need training, so think carefully, and talk it over with the Chinese managers and your help-mate before taking action. The most normal punishments, in ascending order, are a warning, followed by a stern warning; for something really serious it might be possible to impose a fine or demote the worker to a lower grade.

15   Do note that labour-saving is not wanted in China. You should resist all efforts to get you to overstaff which may be made in order to reduce local unemployment. Even if labour becomes scarce locally, the attitude persists, as overmanning seems to have been written into the psyche by decades of large absolute increases in population and the workings of central planning. Nepotism and the hiring of relatives is common and another source of overstaffing.

16   Do note that there is no pool of skilled labour. Even basic skills like driving a car or typing are scarce. You will probably have to train your own workers and then try to hang on to them. It is now easier to hire workers, especially in the Special Economic Zones, to which workers are flocking from other areas. Another problem in the skilled area is that a local engineer may not want to get his hands dirty and it is often impossible to know what the paper qualifications actually mean. Despite this, local engineers are often good.

17   Do note that a boss has social obligations. You will be asked to intervene in personal matters, perhaps as an arbitrator in a dispute (see Chapter 5, Note 21), write letters of recommendation for a staff member's relatives that you do not know, or obtain some scarce (in China) item from abroad for a manager, which action may be dubiously legal. Refusal to help is a serious matter and may cause the staff member to leave.

18   Do watch for a tendency in the joint venture to stockpile produce. During the centrally planned era, all units tried to build up stockpiles of materials and parts, in order to guard against future shortage or late deliveries. They also stockpiled extra output and hid it in order to meet future targets more easily. The habit lingers, and stockpiles tend to build up unless you keep an eye open.

Part Two
Inappropriate Behaviour or What Not to Do

10 General points on proper behaviour

1 Do not be surprised at the ambivalent Chinese attitude towards foreigners. You will be both admired, for being from a country which is rich and with a modern economy, but looked down upon for not being Chinese and hence uncultured. Your normal Western behaviour would underline this for the Chinese (see Chapter 1, Note 26).

2 Do not assume there is one type of 'Chinese' or that all Chinese are the same. The Chinese themselves recognize clear regional differences. Many Chinese have set expectations about their compatriots from other parts of the country. Northerners from around Beijing are seen as phlegmatic, stolid and aloof with a tendency to be dilettantes; the Hunnanese and the Sichuanese are regarded as being fiery and rebellious; the Shanghainese are thought of as devious city-slickers who spend money on good living and fine clothes and care much about their appearance; and the Cantonese are felt to be loud, boisterous, a bit earthy, and not really fully civilized. The Cantonese themselves tend to pride themselves as being the descendants of the 'true' Chinese who were pushed south by northern invaders. The different groups do not subscribe to the stereotype of themselves, of course, and would be hurt to be accused of it. Experience after China opened up has persuaded some foreigners that in contract negotiations the Beijing people are straightforward and easy to deal with, the Shanghainese are cunning but well versed in Western business practice and this makes doing business easier, and the Cantonese are sometimes devious and more care must be taken doing business with them. Individuals vary so much that such generalizations (which may not be true) cannot be accepted as reliable for any particular case.

3 Do not think that the Chinese are the same as the Japanese, with whom you may have experience. They share some elements, such as being cautious in the early stages, looking for long-term relationships, and a preference for indirectness, but are different in other ways. The Chinese tend to base their loyalties on family, but the Japanese on the nation. The Chinese never bow and find Japanese politeness excessive and rather false. China itself is different from Japan, being poor, lacking in infrastructure, skilled labour and modern technology, with little awareness of the need for quality. The Japanese tend to be more racist, formally behaved, traditional in attitude and group-minded. These are just a few of the differences, and it is important not to blindly reproduce in China some things you may have learned from doing business with the Japanese or vice versa.

4   Do not boast or state in a dictatorial way what should or should not be done. Equally, do not be condescending when passing on information or instructions. The latter can be particularly bad, as in Chinese eyes it smacks of racist or colonialist attitudes which, in view of China's history, can upset them greatly. Fortunately, the Chinese are used to foreigners behaving in ways that are considered bad manners, e.g. noisy drunken parties, and make allowances.

5   Do not indulge in loud behaviour or hold noisy parties. It is very bad manners to exhibit noisy, flashy and boisterous behaviour, such as punching playfully on the arm, or boisterous rough-housing play. Such actions appear as extremely offensive, rather than friendly or a part of showing decent enjoyment. Even touching a Chinese should be avoided, other than a handshake. If you feel you have to let off steam, do is as quietly as you can and try not to get drunk in public.

The natural Chinese arrogance of believing that they are innately superior helps you here, for the Chinese simply do not expect inferiors to understand or be able to live up to Chinese values. As a corollary, they are usually very impressed if you do. You should note that it is often not easy to know when you have insulted someone, as they have been trained since birth to conceal their true feelings. If a Chinese person was behaving normally and in friendly fashion but suddenly looks inscrutable and blank, you have probably hurt his or her feelings or insulted them in some way. It is important not to say anything critical of China, 'the Chinese', or any particular Chinese person, as people easily, indeed almost automatically, get offended if you do.

If you manage to develop a real friendship with a Chinese, be careful to avoid friendly rude banter, joshing, critical laughing comments, slapping on the back or even touching the friend. It may seem a mark of true friendship to you but would hurt the recipient. An actual real friendship with a Chinese would probably seem rather austere to you.

6   Do not slump in a chair or put your feet on the table. Be careful about posture and try to sit upright in your chair. Even sitting with crossed legs might be seen as indicating a lack of attention or true concern. You are advised to watch the way the Chinese sit at meetings and copy it. If relaxing in a hotel room, some Westerners might place their feet upon a coffee table when chatting with friends, especially at the end of a long and tiring day sightseeing, etc. This should never be done in front of a Chinese, as it rather disgusts them.

7   Do not stand with your hands on your hips looking down your nose. This seems very arrogant and condescending. You must avoid condescension, especially if explaining something, such as modern technology or how things are done abroad. The latter should be avoided, unless you are asked directly. Great shows of decisive energy may seem like the actions of a dynamic young executive to you, but to the Chinese, this also looks arrogant and aggressive.

8   Do not point with the index finger, or indicate directions with the foot or a jerk of the hand, the way you might do at home. This will often be taken as a sign of scorn. Any person vaguely in line with the direction indicated might well be offended, and everyone around will think you an ill-mannered person. In traditional China it was considered particularly bad to point at a rainbow, as it was felt that a broken finger might result. You should avoid using the foot carelessly. When waiting in a line at an airport, Westerners are likely to nudge their bags forward with the foot or use their foot to reach a dropped pencil and nudge it within reach. Such behaviour, instead of stooping and using the hand, is considered bad-mannered by the Chinese.

9   Do not beckon with the palm uppermost and finger crooked upwards, in Western fashion. If you have to beckon, hold the palm down and wave the fingers towards you.

10   Do not be surprised if the Chinese are badly dressed. Not only is China a poor country but until the end of Maoism in the mid-1970s it was dangerous to stand out. Indulging in different or high-quality clothing could be seen as indicating capitalist tendencies, for which one would be severely punished, or perhaps even killed. Cut off for so many years from the world and the idea of fashion, many Chinese are simply unaware of and

uninterested in clothing fashions or styles, and dress in ways that look crude or unkempt to foreign business people. Their clothes may be ill-fitting and display a complete disregard for colour matching. Among the younger and more yuppy-like Chinese, especially those making large sums of money from the relatively new market sectors, there is, however, an immense desire to wear the latest Western styles. Among this small but wealthy group, conspicuous consumption is the norm and designer labels are often flaunted.

11   Do not be surprised if occasionally you encounter a noisy, inquisitive, rather bossy, middle-aged woman. Such people were once important in the street committees and had immense power over their neighbours. After Maoism ended, they lost their power and function, and some are now bored busybodies with a sense of frustration. If they speak some English and bustle up to you, they can sometimes be helpful by indicating the correct way to the hotel, etc.

12   Do not be surprised if you are stared at or pointed out. Many people who live in the big cities such as Beijing, Shanghai, Tianjin and Guangzhou are used to seeing foreigners, but some are not. These may live in outlying suburbs where foreigners rarely penetrate, or they may have recently arrived from rural China, where foreigners are still rare. If you wander away from the central areas of a city you might find that a crowd gathers to stare or children even follow you. Do not be disconcerted, for there is no malevolence involved. Chinese cities are generally very safe places.

13   Do not be surprised if strangers come up to talk to you. They usually wish to practise their English, but some will offer to change money, especially on the street near big hotels. You are advised not to accept, for it is illegal to do so, and the rate you get is rarely worth the risk of ruining your business prospects. If a stranger asks you to do a favour, be careful, as it may involve doing something which is dangerous or illegal, such as smuggling out a letter. The issue could easily blow up into an international incident with you at the centre. If this occurs, your chances of future business might be reckoned as slim.

14   Do not assume that laughter means happiness. Laughter can, of course, be genuine, but it may also reveal embarrassment and uncertainty of what to do or say if someone has offended an important canon of behaviour, or perhaps had a personal mishap such as tripping and falling over. It is not laughter against you but is used to fill the gap and reveals that they are in a dilemma. Help may not be forthcoming as Chinese often fear to take individual responsibility, and as a foreigner you are something of an unknown quantity. The announcement of a personal tragedy may also cause laughter, apparently acting as a tension-releasing device.

15 Do not say 'I hope you are well'. The Chinese listen carefully to what others say and analyse it, and they are likely to start to wonder why you hope they are well, and may suspect you hope they are not well or why bother to mention it. The use of indirect phrases and hidden meanings means that living in China is not unlike being engaged in permanent office politics at home. A traditional greeting that you might still hear is 'Have you eaten yet?', a reflection of poverty.

16 Do not express surprise if you encounter spitting or noisy throat clearing. Some believe that the flatter Chinese nasal system encourages sinus problems and blockages, others that the dust blowing in the north of China, and the bad air pollution of most Chinese cities, exacerbate sinus problems. Certainly, spitting in China has a long history and spittoons are often provided and used in many institutions, as well as along some streets. Spitting is regarded as a natural body function, even if a trifle unrefined. Try not to let it bother you, do not look disgusted and never complain about it. Should you encounter someone breaking wind loudly, they are probably of low class, as it is considered impolite in company. The common term for it (pronounced 'fang pee') is a very minor swearword that urchins might use.

17 Do not look askance if shouting or noisy behaviour is encountered. In part, it is inherent in the society and language: two Cantonese friends who are getting along famously and enjoying themselves often sound as if they are brawling. Sometimes it is high spirits, and often the noise level is merely the result of the large number of people crowded in cities trying to be heard. China can be a noisy place.

18 Do not display affection publicly. Kissing or cuddling in public are offensive to older Chinese, although many younger ones have begun to do such things, which is a cause of scandal to the mature and elderly. Even kissing your wife in public is better avoided. Under no circumstances should an expat husband or wife allow themselves to become involved emotionally with a Chinese citizen. The usual response by the authorities would be to worry about state security and put the foreigner on an early flight out of China.

19   Do not expect a vast market that will make you instant profits. The lure of the large China market has been around since the middle of the nineteenth century and resurfaced when China began to open up during the 1970s. So far, it has always been an illusion. China provides a good and steadily expanding market, it enjoys high growth rates (about 8–12 per cent per annum in the early 1990s) and these are expected to continue. It still requires effort to make money.

20   Do not tell jokes, especially political ones. Humour does not cross cultural borders easily and what you find amusing will often seem totally unfunny to the Chinese. In particular, you must avoid trying to joke about China, Chinese leaders or government policies. In addition, do not indulge in jokey name-calling or banter, which is rarely understood and merely appears rude.

21   Do not brag about breaking the rules or impish behaviour that you may have practised. This always irritates people, even if you feel that you are endearing yourself by showing you are human and with an ability to circumnavigate restrictions. To many Chinese, this seems a dreadful thing to do and something to be hidden, not a matter for boasting.

22   Do not be surprised if you get tired. There is much that is new and culture shock is quite exhausting. The Chinese work you for long hours and may send you off sightseeing between meetings, while minor infections can drag down your energy level. Some Chinese tend to think of foreigners as rather effete and physically incapable, and it is better not to admit to being tired unless you are exhausted. It merely reinforces their prejudice and they may start to try to use it as a weapon in negotiations.

23   Do not offer to tip, unless one is clearly being demanded. Most Chinese have been told for years about tips being evil, but, especially in new joint-venture hotels, they are learning the benefits of the system. It is often better to give small gifts instead of money and if visiting a Chinese home you should take a gift.

24   Certain items must *not* be given as gifts. These include knives (symbolizing fighting and antagonism), cut flowers (funerals and death), clocks (also death associated), anything pure-white in colour or blue/yellow in combination (death), and anything remotely connected with sex or underwear. Never wrap a present in white paper.

25   Certain topics must *not* be raised by you. Do not discuss sex, Taiwan, human rights, the Cultural Revolution, the relative wealth of the two countries, poor Chinese amenities, Chinese politics, or current or recent Chinese leaders. Mao Zedong and Zhou Enlai are respected, but it is wise to avoid talking about them as you might say the wrong thing. Most Chinese would prefer not to discuss such a dangerous topic as a living or recently deceased leader. You should also avoid saying 'You Chinese', which sounds patronizing or even aggressive.

26 Do not criticize anything you see or hear. The Chinese group feeling and Confucian values encourage conformity, and a criticism of one can be felt by all. A natural antagonism is felt if foreigners criticize one's country, and the Chinese are very patriotic. It is also wise to avoid criticizing your own country and its leaders, as the Chinese find it hard to understand both that you are allowed to do this or would wish to do so. It is also wise to avoid criticizing your own firm or colleagues for similar reasons. The Chinese may question if they should do business with someone who lacks awareness of proper behaviour and may be insincere.

27 Do not refer to Taiwan as a country or say 'the Republic of China', nor include Taiwan in a list of countries. If it must be on a list, you can perhaps call the list 'countries and regions' or add 'and the Chinese Province of Taiwan'. Similarly, avoid the phrase 'Communist China', 'Mainland China' and, of course, 'Red China', all of which will result in consternation and possibly a walk-out by the Chinese side.

28 Do not simply enter a doorway in front of someone, but hang back to let them go first. Expect the Chinese to do the same and put up with a certain amount of jockeying for position.

29 Do not express surprise if you encounter racist attitudes. Many years of Marxist propaganda against racism have fallen on rather deaf ears. A well-known folk story refers to God baking the first people in the oven: some were underdone and turned out white and pasty, some were overdone and burnt black, but with the Chinese they came out a perfect golden brown. Women from Suchow are regarded as the prettiest in China, in part because they are traditionally very pale-skinned. You will see people, women especially, holding up an umbrella or newspaper when crossing a sunny street, even for a few yards, in order to stay as pale as possible. Sunbathing is generally not popular as it darkens the skin.

30 Do not be surprised at the poverty or run-down state of the buildings. China is poor, and for decades the housing stock was allowed to deteriorate badly, largely because rents were set at levels too low to allow for maintenance, although housing maintenance was a low priority of the planners.

31 Do not drink the water. All tap or well water is boiled in China before drinking. Centuries of illness or death as a result of drinking unboiled water have taught the Chinese how unsafe it is. In your hotel, water from the refrigerator is perfectly safe to drink and you can clean your teeth at the tap, but do not drink from it unless it says you can.

32 Do not ask if someone is a Party member. It would embarrass those who are not members but would like to be, while those who are members might start to wonder why you want to know. They will certainly report back the incident and it could lead to you being watched. The secrecy endemic to China precludes such questions.

33 Do not insist that your group splits up to do different things, even if this would be the most efficient way of proceeding, e.g. with engineers looking at machinery while the financial wizard talks to the accountants. The idea alarms the Chinese, who always view a group as having a common interest. The group should also avoid arguing in public or discussing what should be done next – always retire and do such things in private.

34 Do not ever cause someone to 'lose face'. For example, do not criticize a suggestion or reject a proposal, but say that you will consider it (see Chapter 4, Note 9 and Chapter 12, Note 14).

35 Do not ever touch an abacus should you come across one. There may well be a complex sum half-completed sitting on it, so that fiddling with the beads or altering even one can destroy a lot of work.

36 Do not photograph anyone without permission. Northern Chinese in particular may object to being photographed as many believe it brings sorrow. In the south it is different and many Cantonese and boat-people not only do not object but actually wish to be photographed, especially at certain festivals when it is thought to be lucky.

37 Do not thoughtlessly ask a private individual to come to your hotel. It is often very difficult for private people to travel, they have no car, the public transport system is often very crowded, the routes might not be well arranged for the journey, and the bicycle might be needed by some other family member. Naturally, if they live close by or have access to a vehicle it is different. It is better to let them suggest a suitable meeting-place.

38 Do not be surprised if the price you are charged is higher than the locals pay. Many services such as travel and hotel accommodation or telephone installation run on a sliding price scale, with local Chinese having access extremely cheaply, Overseas Chinese paying more, and foreigners paying more again. Foreigners also can be on different rates, e.g. students, expert advisers, tourists, and business people. Resentment over differential pricing easily arises.

39 Do not buy antiques in China unless you are an expert. They are genuine but horrifically expensive. You can legally buy only from designated antique shops for foreigners, and the antiques that you are allowed to export from China have a red sealing-wax blob underneath. You can often buy the same or better items in Hong Kong or Taipei for a fraction of the price. Again, a multi-price system operates, and in ordinary shops (i.e. those not restricted to foreigners) an antique might be only 5–10 per cent of the foreigner-shop price.

40 Avoid some colours and combinations of them. Plain white is always to be avoided (e.g. for a dress, suit or shirt and trousers), as these are close to traditional mourning garments. Blue and white together, or blue and yellow together, also suggest death and are best avoided; at a funeral a gift would often be placed in a yellow envelope with a blue stripe. A green hat should also be avoided, as to many Chinese it suggests a cuckolded person.

11 Approaching China

1   Do not be surprised if a letter gets no response, as the Chinese feel no obligation towards strangers, who are not an 'insider' or part of their network or system (see Chapter 1, Note 9).

2   Do not send someone too young. Confucian values take 30 years as the age of proper maturity, and below that one is not easily taken seriously in business or politics. The Chinese hierarchical view of the world also means that senior people are automatically taken more seriously.

3   Do not send a person with an unsuitable appearance. Long wavy hair and a moustache are undesirable, as they are a standard way in theatre and film of portraying the image of an insincere villain. In Western eyes he would be the sort of Western movie banker who menaces the heroine by threatening to foreclose on the farm. Anyone with a hawk-like nose and thin eyebrows is also quite unsuitable, as they suggest cunning liars of treacherous disposition. Trust can be hard to build up, especially if to the other people you look exactly like a diabolical pirate.

4   Do not send anyone who is likely to be heavy-handed, arrogant, impatient, rigid, tense, racist, aloof, or loud. All such attitudes or behavioural tendencies jar heavily and mitigate against doing well in China. What you need are sensitive people, who get along with foreign strangers, who are warm and outgoing but in a quiet way. Flexibility in approach and good reserves of energy are desirable.

5   Do not send a lone person, as you will forfeit respect, since traditionally a leader does not engage in nuts-and-bolts negotiating, and needs advisers. A single person will be heavily outnumbered and unlikely to be able to answer all the questions asked. Finally, he might become mentally exhausted having no one with whom to relax or let off steam.

6   Do not change members of your team if it can be avoided. The Chinese wish to see you as 'old friends' and this need would be violated. In practical terms, it might slow down negotiations if the Chinese commence delaying in order to get to know the new members, whom they will not automatically trust.

7   Do not despair if you keep being asked if yours is the best product or technology, even though the Chinese will not reveal what the problem is that they are trying to solve or why they really need the technology or item. The questioning is a reflection of the Chinese wanting the best, but at the same time being hemmed in by a desire for secrecy, an unwillingness to expose internal matters to 'outsiders' and an unsureness if orders from above will change.

8   Do not be afraid of making mistakes and committing solecisms, despite this list of 'Do nots'. The Chinese expect you as a barbarian to do strange things, and easily forgive you for being a foreigner and not knowing better. If you are constantly worried, it will impact adversely on your negotiating power, so try to relax. 'Take it easy' is good advice.

9   Do not use sexy advertising, which is unacceptable at present, although this is relaxing a little. Equally, do not use pushy aggressive adverts, as these strike a negative chord in the Chinese. Also note that free samples have not proved to be very successful as a promotion device.

12   *Meetings and negotiations*

1   Do not be late for appointments. It is extremely rude to be late for any appointment, even for a sightseeing trip. This is partly, but not entirely, because it is polite in China to have someone standing by to meet and escort you, so you are tying up that person's time. Being unpunctual is considered far worse than in the West, where it is merely impolite.

2   Do not start trying to negotiate the day you arrive. You will be tired, probably jet-lagged and not fit to make decisions. In any case, you should never sit down and start to talk business in the early stages, as it will frighten and alienate the Chinese, who will assume you are merely a crass barbarian, totally lacking in an appreciation of proper behaviour. At this early stage, you are not trying to sell your product, you are trying to establish the idea of you and your firm being sound and reliable.

3   Do not ignore any member of the Chinese team, as it is rarely (if ever) clear who has responsibility for what. Remember, everyone involved has to agree in order to make a deal but it takes only one person to stop it. A quiet self-effacing person in the corner might have more real power than anyone else in the room. You should not automatically assume that the leader, the most senior person present, has the most power.

4   Do not ever use a Chinese person's given name. It is tempting, especially if Australian or American, to start to use the Christian or given name when addressing someone, as in those societies it suggests friendliness and informality, helping to cement a business relationship. Never do this in China as it would be extremely rude and actually drive a powerful wedge into the relationship. Eventually, if you get to know a Chinese well, he might ask you to use his initials, which is a common mode of address among friends, but you must never do so unless asked.

5   Do not sit an Overseas Chinese next to your leader, as this is where the interpreter usually sits. If you do this, the Chinese will see him or her as merely an interpreter, and as such the person will be considered to have lowly status and not be a full member of your team. Your Overseas Chinese colleague would lose face and the Chinese themselves would not listen to what he or she has to suggest. Although Overseas Chinese make good interpreters, and there is a clear cost saving by using, for example, an Overseas Chinese engineer in this role, it is dangerous to do so. The Overseas Chinese can help with technical phrases, of course, making it clear that this is merely to help everyone present to understand.

6   Do not take the 'honoured seat' unless asked. This seat faces the door, with its back to a wall. It is regarded as the best seat, probably because in earlier and more violent times sitting there prevented someone sneaking in to attack from behind. To be seated there was a guarantee that the host would not attack and kill you, or at least was not making it easy for himself.

7   Do not excessively prune your 'brief introduction' which is delivered at the first meeting. Both sides make such an introduction the ice-breaker. You need to explain clearly who is on your team and with what function (although the Chinese will rarely do this for you), how your firm is organized, what markets you sell in, etc. Your aim is to impress them that you and your firm are reliable, important, able to deliver, and well regarded in your country and, if possible, internationally.

8   Do not drink too much tea in a meeting. Be careful not to overdo it and strain your bladder, as there seem to be few 'comfort breaks'. The reason is probably that the host would probably prefer you not to see the state of the lavatories in most institutions that are not designed for foreigners. Chinese plumbing is often deficient, Asian-style toilets are common (no pedestal, just a hole in the floor), and where there is a pedestal, it is often forbidden to place used toilet paper in it as this blocks the pipes, so that a bucket is provided at the side for the paper. It would embarrass the host to have to explain this fact to you, and he would probably feel that it reflected badly on China and the institution itself. In any case, the Chinese are adept at sipping tea for hours without apparent discomfort.

9   Do not assume that the people around do not speak English and particularly do not engage in criticism or make jocular remarks at the expense of the Chinese. If you do, it is embarrassing if after some time the person next to you suddenly addresses you in English.

10 Do not show anxiety or impatience in early meetings which tend to go slowly and seem to achieve little. This is normal.

11 Do not be pushy or try aggressively to speed up the pace of negotiations, as not only will you almost certainly fail, but you might convince the Chinese that you are a dubious proposition. The Western concept of aggressive competition, including details like power dressing, can let you down in the Chinese milieu. Harmony and consensus are sought. You might find that efforts to speed things up actually backfire, as the Chinese may respond by deliberately slowing the pace down.

12 Try not to talk fast and engage in high-pressure salesmanship, which is quite inappropriate and will annoy the Chinese. It is at odds with their approach of harmony, etc. and they dislike the fast-talking, 'snake-oil salesman' approach.

13 Do not promise more than you can deliver. The Chinese might tempt you to do so by indicating that if you do something they want, the contract is likely to go to you. You should be careful not to promise something that you think you can swing back home, without being certain of it. The Chinese note all concessions carefully and will remind you of them and expect you to honour your word.

14 Do not say 'no'. If it is impossible to agree, a way around is to say that you will think it over carefully and let them know, or discuss it with your colleagues after the meeting or in detail with the important people in your company headquarters, etc. It is quite acceptable to say that you will take it on board and that it can be discussed at a later stage. The Chinese themselves do this constantly. Note that 'It will be difficult' or 'It will not be easy' generally mean 'no' to a Chinese, rather than a statement of fact. You should avoid a blunt 'no', as it means a strong loss of face for the recipient.

15 Do not think a nod means 'yes'. It usually indicates 'I am awake and listening' or 'please continue', and there is no agreement signified for what you are saying.

16 Do not be surprised if silence greets an awkward question; they are either embarrassed or it is a way of saying 'no'. Do not feel that you have to talk to break a silence and try not to let a protracted silence get on your nerves (see Chapter 5, Note 5).

17 Do not force a showdown or deliver an ultimatum, as this is almost always counterproductive. Always try to leave a door open for negotiations. Do not try to force them to divulge information in discussions. If you really need to know something, you could try writing down the request and transmitting it to the Chinese side, via a go-between such as the contact person or an interpreter, preferably giving it to that person when alone. This avoids any loss of face but communicates what you wish to the Chinese side. If things get desperate, the Chinese will understand that you need more concessions, if you make it clear you are about to leave China without an agreement. This is a form of acceptable ultimatum, but is not done openly as a threat.

18 Do not be surprised if you are faced with an unacceptable demand. You should not reject a preposterous suggestion out of hand but discuss it. They could be using it as a ploy, as something to give up in order to get a concession from you. It could be a signal that they wish to stop negotiations and are trying to force you to break them off. If you are faced with this situation, it helps to say that you will report back to headquarters for guidance (if you are not a one-person firm) as this keeps the negotiations open. A blunt 'no' should be avoided, unless you have decided to cut your losses and leave. If you reach that stage, it is worth informing the Chinese that you are considering leaving, doing this through an intermediary, and they might back down, depending on how seriously they wish to do business with you.

19 Do not interrupt anyone, as it demonstrates arrogance as well as breaking up harmony and interfering with the growing relationship. You set your cause back by interrupting, however much you feel the urge. Calm patience is needed; you will get your turn.

20 Do not invent a figure off the top of your head, even for illustrative purposes to use as an example. It will be noted down and may be used against you in later negotiations, as a cost or price that you offered. This may be partly the result of poor interpretation, but if you float hypothetical figures in this way it fits awkwardly in the culture and is often taken to be an indirect genuine offer and believed. It can also be raised later as a deliberate ploy, and the Chinese with their attention to detail and scrupulous record-keeping might point out that you yourself said it, and demand that you keep your word. Never try to speak 'off the record' either, as it will not be off the record even if they agree it is. It is normal practice for a Chinese to report back to his organization (as an insider) what you (the outsider) have indicated, whether you said it at a formal session or when you were at leisure.

21 Do not expect quick decisions. The slow nature of the workings of the bureaucracy, the Chinese caution and fear of being

exploited, the desire to build up relationships with you, and the fact that parallel negotiations may be continuing with other foreign firms mean that time can pass with little to show. Do not be surprised if the Chinese apparently think that you can stay and negotiate for ever. Time sometimes seems of little concern to the Chinese and you may encounter deliberate use of go-slow tactics.

22 Do not be surprised to meet insecurity or uncertainty among the Chinese. It can be based on several factors, including their leader being new to the job, an awareness of past foreign exploitation of China and fear that they will be deceived, unclear orders from above on what is expected of them, a change in the local power structure that is leaving them more vulnerable, or a fear that a major policy change may render the negotiations pointless.

23 Do not show impatience or anger, which is not only a sign of childish weakness in China but will be taken advantage of to be used against you where possible. Avoid confrontation, and never slam your hand or fist on the table, break a pencil in anger or hit things in frustration.

24 Do not be surprised to meet anger from the Chinese. If during negotiations you find that a Chinese gets angry, you should assume that it is feigned and part of their tactics, perhaps to see how you respond. If anyone stridently lectures you on your or your country's behaviour, or even slams out of the room, ask yourself why they are doing this at that point. Be careful not to get angry or even impatient, but explain calmly and politely why what they demand is extremely difficult. You can be persistent, even relentless, but this must be in a context of calm rationality. Some people advocate a calculated occasional loss of temper by you, but this is a dangerous form of negotiating and is usually better avoided.

25 Do not be surprised if you are made to feel guilty or are called 'unfriendly'. It is common practice to try to make you feel shame or guilt for your behaviour; your country's domestic or political actions; or your company's refusal to help them more. Traditionally, causing an opponent to feel shame was both pursued and effective, because of the importance of 'face'. Your best response is to be polite and dignified. Point out that a nation's politics are not your concern; if China is ever criticized, the Chinese are quick to point out that internal politics are not a matter for foreigners, and you can echo this point of view if it helps. Try not to blame yourself if the negotiations are not going well.

26 Do not be surprised if the Chinese refuse things of benefit to them. It usually means that they are being ultra-cautious and stalling, possibly because they have not yet finished assessing you and have not yet learned to trust you and suspect a trap, or possibly because of confused signals, or lack of instructions, coming from above. Without higher approval, nothing can happen.

27 Do not be surprised if the Chinese keep returning to a topic and discussing it again. They seem to believe in the theory of perpetual negotiations. Do not worry if the Chinese re-open negotiations and ask for changes after a contract has been agreed and signed. Never assume that you have finished once it is signed and do not get irritated when the Chinese raise the question of amendments (see Chapter 5, Notes 18–20). Since what is considered rude varies between societies, you might feel that a particular Chinese is being ill-mannered when he or she presses hard for detailed information or keeps returning to a point and discussing it again. It is not thought particularly rude in China to do this when negotiating with foreigners.

28 Do not criticize a Chinese publicly as this would cause an extreme loss of face to him or her and you would not be forgiven or receive his or her support henceforth. Indeed, the person would be more inclined to oppose whatever seemed to be in your best interest. If when working in China you must reprimand a staff member, take the person into your office quietly and do it tactfully, suggesting ways that performance might be improved. Rather than criticizing and telling him not to do something, suggest that an alternative way might work better and ask him to try it.

29 Do not concede anything too easily. Despite the recommended approach of staying calm, smiling and being friendly, it is important to be a firm negotiator and not give in easily. You should be well prepared, know what you can give up, what your costs are, and what your fall-back position is. The Chinese have a well-deserved reputation for negotiating and can sweep you along. Be particularly careful not to make a series of individual concessions, each small in its own right but adding up to a significant loss. This is a well-known tactic in China, where some call it 'ants gnawing away at a bone'. If you are suddenly hit with a request you have not previously considered, do not agree to it, but ask for it to be considered later, thus gaining time to think through the implications.

30 Do not aim to be cosily friendly with the Chinese team, as this might limit your ability to be tough when needed. Although they may appear friendly, they are primarily doing their job, which is to gain the best for China at the least possible cost.

31 Do not take the 'friendship' remarks too seriously. Although the Chinese are often sincere when talking about friendship, it can be nothing more than a polite phrase that seems appropriate at the time (see Chapter 4, Note 26).

32 Do not be alarmed if the Chinese suddenly stop negotiating or, alternatively, announce that they are ready to sign a contract even before all the details are thrashed out. Sometimes these are ploys to increase tension and uncertainty. Despite the statement, a signature may not be forthcoming. At other times such sudden changes may reflect intensified pressure from higher levels or a change in policy direction and therefore is genuine.

33 Do not think that a 'memorandum of understanding', 'letter of intent' or 'protocol' is binding in any way. You will often find pressure on you to sign one of these. You should always agree to do this and recall that it is not a contract in the Western sense. It is quite common for foreigners to regard an agreement as having been signed, when it is merely the start of the Chinese process of negotiation. Be careful not to make any negative noises at this stage, even if you know something cannot be done – this is a matter for later when details are discussed.

34 Do keep your expectations private and do not talk to the press. The Chinese side often keeps the negotiations quiet but you might find that they encourage you to go public when you sign an early memorandum of understanding, etc. If you do this, and many do, it is harder for you subsequently to break off negotiations and face public embarrassment. This is particularly so if your CEO went to China and signed a memorandum of understanding, publicized it internationally, then left the detailed negotiations to underlings, as often happens. If you do break off negotiations, it is not only embarrassing but your CEO is also likely to want to know why you could not negotiate something he had agreed in principle. Once the final contract is signed you can publicize it safely.

35 Do not automatically believe statements that you have a good chance of winning a competitive contract, etc. as it is not unknown for every firm in the running to be told the same. It has proved an effective tactic for gaining concessions. Do not be surprised if an attempt is made to play you off against a competitor.

36 Do not automatically accept a model contract. Standard contracts exist, but they tend to favour the Chinese on things like shipping dates and penalties, and also exclude much detail you might need. Do not accept at face value a statement that such is the only possible contract that can be approved, for this is a negotiating ploy. Never rely on verbal agreements either, but get what you want on paper somewhere in the contract.

37 Do not worry if you seem to be caught between different government organizations, for there is a long history of their refusal to cooperate with each other. In China, every other institute is an 'outsider' to be mistrusted and cooperation is to be avoided. You should also anticipate little lateral communication will exist, as reports and instructions go up and down, but few units communicate with others at their own level. Do not overlook the uncertainty and delay caused by this lack of cooperation between overlapping government levels and units. With the decentralization and rather chaotic situation caused by rapid change, it is important also not to overestimate the day-to-day role and power of the central government. Remember, however, that in the end it has absolute power.

38 Do not set your prices too far above international ones, as the Chinese routinely check such things. They are not short of people to undertake detailed investigations of a mundane kind. You need some padding, but not more than they will accept as a reasonable starting position. You should not be surprised if the Chinese argue strongly about price. Be particularly careful not to specify a price early in negotiations, even off the top of your head as a hypothetical example.

39 Do not rely on current prices remaining unchanged. If you do your sums on present prices you might get a nasty shock if the price of your raw materials suddenly increases. In China, if and when state-set prices are changed to market prices, they can increase several-fold. You should remember to ask if the prices that are being used in any feasibility studies are freely floating market prices or are set by the state in some way.

40 Do not talk about prices until you know exactly what is involved and what you will be expected to do. There may be unacknowledged expenses you will be expected to meet, such as training schemes, the provision of manuals, or a trip to Beijing or even to your country.

41 Do not use slang while negotiating. As in all dealings with people from other countries, you should avoid colloquial expressions or words from a third language, such as 'getting the show on the road', 'looking at the bottom line', 'déjà vu' or 'in extremis'.

Likewise, avoid irony and sarcasm, as there is a better than even chance that the words will be translated directly and then believed to represent your view.

42   Do not rely solely on a high-level contact, as that is not where the actual recommendations are made. You should start at the top when seeking something, then use what influence you can from that level to help you when negotiating later lower down. You should not be surprised, however, if an agreement made by a top institution fails to be carried out, as units have been known to change their minds. Do not be surprised if you face an unexpected meeting with a high official; the Chinese sometimes wheel one out to try to impress you and increase the pressure on you to make a concession.

43   Do not try to establish *guanxi* with a very senior official who is well beyond your level. It comes down to a question of hierarchy and rank. Relationships work on a *quid pro quo* basis, and (unless you are a Chinese and a protégé of someone) usually take place between people of reasonably similar rank. As there is probably nothing you could do for him or her in return, a high-level official will know this and might feel insulted that you tried to enmesh him or her. Just be friendly and polite.

44   Do not be surprised if the negotiating power of the Chinese side alters. Often at the start, they seem to have full negotiating power, but later you may realize that they have not. In part, it may be a matter of 'face' and a negotiator trying to impress by pretending access to central power. In part, it may be a tactic to see what they can squeeze out, knowing that when you ask for something major in return they can suspend the meetings in order to seek instructions from above and reveal their limitations at that point.

45   Do not agree to important matters being put in the appendix of the contract. That is the place for the details and perhaps expanding the main principles agreed; all important matters and principles should appear in the main body of the text.

46   Do not give expensive gifts, unless one is clearly requested. Large gifts to individuals should be avoided as they smack of bribery and since the Chinese will feel an obligation to repay the gift, something like an automatic camera or notebook computer puts an onus on him or her that cannot possibly be repaid. You should be aware, however, that attitudes in this area are changing rapidly and larger personal gifts are becoming more acceptable. It is quite proper to present a large gift to the whole organization rather than to a person. If, however, you are clearly being asked for a large personal gift, in effect as a bribe, then you must do as your conscience dictates. Many Hong Kong business people are very skilful at making large gifts in a suitably quiet and back-stage manner, in order to gain business.

47   Do not spring a surprise to try to gain an advantage. The Chinese dislike surprises, so if you suddenly announce something new and different, they will normally merely take it on-board and report back at a later meeting. It is better to put a suggestion in writing before the meeting, as any new proposal has to go through collective consideration and decision behind the scenes.

48   Do not gloat or act like a winner. In Chinese eyes this would be terribly bad manners, and they would feel that they had lost something. Their leader might also fear that an opponent might report this to superiors and suggest that a team under his or her leadership could have done better. This would cause the leader immense problems in the normal Chinese office infighting and in his eyes you would share some of the blame for the situation, which bodes badly for future cooperation with you.

49   Do not forget that you need to get profits out of China. This principle and perhaps the mechanism should appear in the contract.

50   Do not hesitate to cut your losses and leave if this is necessary. If you have done your sums, know what costs and prices you can live with, and during the negotiations if it becomes clear that you cannot achieve a profitable situation, you should consider leaving. Only a large firm with reserves can afford to take current losses and hope for future business that will be profitable. The Chinese take a long-term view but you must consider whether it is worth losing money now on a gamble of future profits. Many foreign firms hang on, eventually making money, but given the cost of visiting China, the negotiating time, the probable need to return to keep things moving and so on, it is not always clear that it has been worth the trouble. Other firms obviously do well, because they did not accept a losing situation based on hopes for the future.

13 Socializing and proper behaviour

1 Do not turn down any invitation to lunch, dinner, etc. If the Chinese invite you, they have a reason and it is part of the system. Turning down such an invitation, unless you are really ill, upsets the system and they are then unsure what to do.

2 Do not expect Chinese wives to be present at a banquet. Traditionally, a wife ate apart from her husband, although this did not apply to the poorest section of society. Everyone present at a banquet will be business-oriented, although one or two may be receiving a pay-back for a favour and have relatively little to do with you. If women are present and name cards have not been provided, you might find they try to sit together. You should never ask a Chinese why he has not brought his spouse. If you are in China with your spouse, and he or she is specifically invited, they can and should attend. If you do meet someone's wife, it is incorrect to compliment her on her beauty, which would seem impertinent. Compliment something she does instead, such as cooking beautifully or speaking English well.

3 Do not misuse chopsticks. It is wrong to spear food with one chopstick, even in desperation. You should not point at anyone or thing with your chopsticks, nor wave them about or gesticulate with them while talking. Foreigners tend to do this, probably because having finally managed to hold them properly, they are often reluctant to let them go. Put the chopsticks down first if you tend to wave your arms when you talk.

4 Do not leave any rice in your personal bowl at the end of the meal. It is a cardinal sin to take more rice than you need and then leave some; you should ensure that every last grain of rice is eaten from your personal bowl.

5 Do not lay chopsticks across your bowl at a formal dinner. In a good restaurant, at the end of the meal you should place your chopsticks on the small rest provided, rather than laying them across the rice bowl, which is not the best of manners. In cheap restaurants with no rests provided, then you might see chopsticks laid across the bowl.

6 Do not stick your chopsticks upright in the rice and leave them sticking up. It is very bad to do this, as it symbolizes death. By association, you should not stick them into any dish and leave them standing upright. Recall that many Chinese are superstitious.

7 Do not ask for a knife, even if you cannot use chopsticks, as it is a symbol of violence at the table and unsettling. You will not need one as the food is cut small in the kitchen for eating with chopsticks anyway. Asking for a fork and spoon is quite acceptable and are the commonly used implements in South-east Asia. You might be given a knife anyway, as they know you do not know better.

8 Do not look surprised if someone slurps soup or tea, which is not considered to be bad-mannered.

9 Do not look surprised if someone picks up the bowl to eat from (see Chapter 6, Note 4).

10 Do not raise business issues at a banquet. You might find that the Chinese do so, and they may be trying to take advantage of the relaxed atmosphere or the alcohol you have drunk, to gain an edge. They never really cease negotiating, and if you promise to do something while at the meal, it will be raised at a future meeting as a commitment.

11 Do not point a teapot spout at anyone when putting the pot down. It is a common superstition that it will cause a quarrel between the pair of you and the opposing team might feel uneasy about doing further business.

12 Do not chat in English among yourselves. This would in itself be bad manners and leave the Chinese isolated with no opportunity to participate. It can also be dangerous if you become a little indiscreet and, unknown to you, someone at the table actually speaks fluent English and hears every word.

13 Do not hang around after a banquet or expect after-dinner entertainment, despite it being relatively early. You will normally return to your hotel where, of course, you may go to the bar. Some discos, bars and nightclubs now operate, especially in the major cities and Shenzhen, but they can be rather dreary with an old-fashioned feel. Karaoke bars are currently very popular.

14 Do not strongly admire anything in a Chinese home, as the host might feel obliged to present it to you. As they will be much poorer than you, this would be embarrassing. You should admire and praise the meal if one is served, or the decor as a whole, the way the furniture is arranged to give a feeling of space, etc., but not individual objects.

14 Living and managing in China

1   Do not send a lone expat to live in China. He will face culture shock and find it hard to survive on his own, cut off from normal surroundings and friends. Dealing with teams of Chinese is also tiring on one's own.

2   Do not expect a lot of privacy. It is partly an attitude of mind, associated with the importance of the group not the individual in China, and partly the result of long-standing overcrowding. In addition, for some decades, neighbours have been encouraged to watch each other and report on behaviour and the comings and goings of visitors. The Chinese may behave in ways that you feel infringe your privacy. They are very interested in people and think it quite acceptable to pick up a private letter addressed to you and read it, and you might find that some will enter your room without first knocking. Most hotels have now managed to train their staff not to do this. Individualism is not regarded highly in China and indeed is often a subject of disapproval. Apart from one's hotel room, it is difficult to be alone.

3   Do not jump straight into a joint venture, but consider all the options. It often pays to start with a simple contract to buy or sell. In this way you can learn the ropes, make contacts, visit different factories, judge who might make a good partner, and get to feel comfortable in China. This slow approach costs much less, and you do not have to put so much money up-front. Further down the track, a joint venture might be the way to go, but they can be costly in terms of investment, with a long learning curve to get used to Chinese conditions.

4   Do not agree to an all-Chinese board of management, and try to get over half the numbers on the board if possible. If you have control, problem solving later will prove easier. It is also desirable if you, not the Chinese, control all operating procedures for later troubleshooting purposes.

5   Do not assume that all normal Western facilities will be either needed or available. In China there will be no need for a huge car parking lot but a bicycle storage area will be essential. Electricity might be erratic in supply and have fluctuating voltage, while water and gas supplies can be equally unreliable.

6   Do not be surprised to find that you must pay more than state-owned firms for your fuel, raw materials, water, electricity and telephone use.

7   Do not expect your goals and the Chinese ones to be the same. Yours will be narrower (mainly profit and sales), while the Chinese ones may be wider (see Chapter 3, Note 27).

8   Do not address important officials familiarly. China is a heavily structured society and proper respect must be shown to those higher up. It is important never to talk to an ambassador, for example, as if he or she were an ordinary mortal and an equal. You might feel that he is charming and an equal, but he will feel that you are impertinent if you address him as one. Egalitarianism has little (if any) place in China, despite the political rhetoric since 1949. High officials expect due deference, which they get in abundance from their own people.

9   Do not try to establish an egalitarian system in your company in China or treat the workers as equals. This would be a source of scandal and resentment among the workers and could easily demoralize the Chinese management.

10 Do not agree to a factory layout with lots of small office cubicles. Chinese workers have become used to sleeping, chatting, reading newspapers and playing cards in the office; if possible, go for open-plan, which renders this more difficult.

11 Do not split the joint venture between cities in any way or you will create endless problems of control as well as logistical difficulties of supply and marketing. Worse, you will face inter-city rivalry and might be forced to split your production between regions and thereby lose economies of scale.

12 Do not expect good quality control. The central planning system and decades of sellers' markets have virtually ended quality as a factor in production. Chinese workers do not fully appreciate that international markets demand high quality. You will have to train people to take it seriously, and constantly monitor them to ensure that they do not backslide. In this endeavour, do not become angry but persist in a calm fashion (see Chapter 9, Note 7).

13 Do not expect that equipment will automatically be properly looked after. You might easily find, for example, that exposed machinery or valuable materials will not be covered when it rains. In the past, such things were communal property and were not the responsibility of any particular person. The fact that the machinery is being damaged is clearly seen, but this is not recognized as a problem for the person who sees it nor a matter for them to deal with. You will have to issue instructions to cover such eventualities.

14 Do not expect much in the way of innovation, lateral thinking or creativity among the workers. They can be trained to do a good job, although this requires time and patience, but they tend to do exactly what they are told and no more. Keep checking to see if new instructions have become necessary in the light of operating experience.

15 Do not be surprised if good workers in your joint venture are recalled by the state. The officials may wish to put them in state-owned factories in order to raise the average quality there and try to use them to train others. If this occurs, you then have to train more workers to replace the lost ones. Increasingly, joint ventures can hire their own workers directly and this reduces the danger of workers being recalled.

16 Do not ever fire the son or daughter or a close relative of a powerful local official. Nepotism is common in China and a person is expected to look after his family. The press regularly criticizes the phenomenon but to no avail. If you do sack someone with a powerful relative, he will probably take revenge upon you and your firm in a variety of ways, some petty but irritating, others very damaging. This will cost you far more than you would lose from keeping a bad worker.

17 Do not get annoyed if 'internal rules' are cited at you. They do exist and the passion for secrecy, together with the 'insider/outsider' attitude, mean you cannot even be told that there is such a rule, let alone what it says, even quietly, until you have broken it. Sometimes the Chinese will claim that there is a rule preventing something if they actually do not wish to do it.

18 Do not get upset if the bureaucracy does not inform you of something. It is usually inefficiency rather than a deliberate ploy, but sometimes it may be an individual bureaucrat protecting his back. In China it is always safer not to say something that should be said than actually to say something that should not be said.

19 Do not try to introduce a Chinese from one ministry or area of government to another. It tends to embarrass them, for it seems wrong for an outsider, and a foreign one at that, to know more about the workers of the bureaucracy and its personnel than they do. They may feel a distinct loss of 'face' as a result and you will be blamed for this.

20 Do not hesitate to 'use the back door' if you need something. 'Going through the back door' means using pull, influence and contacts to get what you want, rather than doing it the formal, probably bureaucratic, way. Officially frowned upon, it remains a normal way of doing business, in government, commercial and industrial circles.

15 How to treat visitors to one's own country

1 Do not serve large steaks and slabs of meat, if entertaining at home. Pork is the favourite meat of most Chinese, and poultry is fine, but avoid lamb or mutton, which many Asians find both smells and tastes disgusting. Fish and seafood are always very acceptable to the Chinese. Remember the normal courtesies and seating arrangements.

2 Do not hold barbecues when entertaining. Almost all Chinese are uncomfortable at barbecues, which are an alien concept and they tend to find them threatening. The newness, the informality, the lack of recognizable hierarchy, strangers coming up to address them unannounced and uninvited and the large (and disliked) huge pieces of steak, etc. all seem particularly unpleasant. If you are ill-advised enough to hold a welcoming barbecue, you will probably find that they stand in a silent group, and are rather unresponsive. Basically they feel threatened and out of their depth.

3 Do not forget to begin the toasting when entertaining in a restaurant, as this is a duty of the host. The first toast should be to the guests. You should keep supplying guests with food, so watch carefully and if in a good Chinese restaurant, which is a safe choice of venue, never let their personal bowl get empty. In China it is customary to settle the bill after all the guests have departed and never in their presence. You might prefer to go quietly over to the desk to pay, rather than lay a credit card or cash on the table in front of everyone, as you would normally do.

Part Three
Summary of What to Do

16 General points on proper behaviour

1   Do note that China retains many Confucian values.
2   Do remember that China is in a state of transition and rapid change.
3   Do be aware that facilities in China continue to improve rapidly.
4   Do note that this pace of change brings high stress levels and that changes can be abrupt.
5   Do be aware that the government is autocratic and, although benign, it can be ruthless.
6   Do note that the Chinese are intensely patriotic.
7   Do understand that the Chinese are family and group oriented.
8   Do note that your group needs a strong, identifiable leader.
9   Do remember the importance of the 'insider–outsider' difference.
10 Do note that the Chinese feel no obligation to reply to letters.
11 Do remember China is a hierarchical society and rank counts for much.
12 Do note that the Chinese tend to like the best and go for prestige.
13 Do observe that harmony is sought.
14 Do notice that good manners means being self-deprecating.
15 Do recognize that most Chinese are superstitious and that numbers and colours may have certain connotations.
16 Do observe that the Chinese tend to stand close to you.
17 Eye contact is important although it can mislead, and smiles can mean anger or embarrassment.
18 Do take warm clothing for winter wear and note that Chinese clothing sizes may be too small for you.
19 Do expect to encounter a lot of cigarette smoking.
20 Do buy medicines in Hong Kong before entering China.
21 Do expect a long lunch-time rest period.
22 Do note that a six-day working week is the norm.
23 Do note that the Chinese mostly have three names and, if possible, you should address them by their title.
24 Do note that travel and sightseeing are tiring.

25   Do expect to wait around the hotel a lot or be sent on sight-seeing trips.
26   Do expect to feel that you are a foreigner and note that the Chinese are ambivalent about foreigners.
27   Do note that the Chinese have a view of other nationalities often based on an unpleasant historical relationship.
28   Do clap back if you are applauded.
29   Do recall that China is a secretive society.
30   Do note that using the telephone is difficult.
31   Do expect transport problems and bad traffic conditions.
32   Do be prepared to be constantly asked standard questions, some of them personal.
33   Do remember the safe and unsafe topics of conversation.
34   Do expect restaurants to close early.
35   Do expect to be frustrated in China.

17 Approaching China

1 Do select a good Chinese name for yourself and your product.
2 Do make initial contact properly by mail in the correct fashion.
3 Do use a liaison officer, or help-mate, preferably Chinese.
4 Do have your business card in both English and Chinese.

Who to send

5 Do send an experienced, older person with expertise who is a friendly and sensitive type, and a full team.
6 Do send an Overseas Chinese if possible but note that there could be problems.
7 Do learn a few greeting phrases.
8 Do remember that face-to-face negotiations are essential.
9 Do try to be poised, self-controlled, and use 'soft-sell' tactics.
10 Do expect to be met at the airport or at any organization you are visiting.

18   Meetings and negotiations

1   Do endeavour to check that you are dealing with the appropriate organization.
2   Do note that the host organization determines your status.
3   Do approach your host organization for all requests.
4   Do anticipate that your host organization may not make proper arrangements with other units.
5   Do speak clearly and concisely when negotiating.
6   Do be punctual.
7   Do be attentive to detail.
8   Do expect that if you ask a question, you may receive a question in reply.
9   Do note that the Chinese worry about making mistakes and being exploited.
10   Do notice that the Chinese may adopt an informal approach outside meetings.

Early meetings

11   Do send your material well in advance.
12   Do learn the Chinese names before the meeting.
13   Do expect you will go to a special meeting room, not an ordinary office.
14   Do identify the leader and greet him or her first.
15   Do note that the Chinese always list people in protocol order.
16   Do observe that there is a set protocol for meetings.
17   Do read their business cards slowly and carefully.
18   Do expect three-hour meetings and probably a two-hour break for lunch.
19   Do expect to drink lots of tea and listen to bland introductions.
20   Do expect that the first and early meetings in a series will be formal and go slowly.

21   Do note that the Chinese assess you from the start.
22   Do listen carefully in the early stages.
23   Do take careful notes of what is discussed or decided.
24   Do take your own interpreter.
25   Do use the interpreter to gain maximum benefit.
26   Do note that in negotiating, general principles are laid down first.
27   Do note that the Chinese may see problems differently.

19 Meetings and negotiations – your tactics

1 Do recall that you are working for a long-term relationship.
2 Do note that negotiations can take a long time.
3 Do expect the bureaucracy to be slow and not always helpful.
4 Do expect to encounter rivalry between organizations.
5 Do expect marathon negotiations with little rest.
6 Do be patient, polite and dignified and avoid rudeness.
7 Do be honest and sincere and tell the truth.
8 Do persevere and persist.
9 Do be very careful not to cause a loss of face.
10 Do try to do small favours and develop a relationship.
11 Do treat bureaucrats sympathetically.
12 Do give the shortest reply possible when negotiating.
13 Do look for a concealed 'no'.
14 Do look for indirect signals.
15 Do enquire after China's problems that may be relevant to you.
16 Do keep a written list of your goals and expected costs and be aware of the value of intangibles and your know-how.
17 Do set your price and allow some leeway.
18 Do keep repeating your needs clearly.
19 Do recap what has been agreed at the end of each meeting.
20 Do note that it is easy to misjudge how well negotiations are proceeding.
21 Do consider using a 'go-between' to transmit bad news.
22 Do stand firm when you reach your last position and be prepared to walk away.
23 Do observe that the Chinese want the latest technology rather than preserving jobs.
24 Do take many gifts but choose them carefully.
25 Do accept that you may need to invite the Chinese to visit your country or pay for a local trip for the Chinese.
26 Do send the same personnel each time if possible.
27 Do expect to be treated rather like a supplicant to a powerful emperor.
28 Do send a senior person to conclude the negotiations.

20 Meetings and negotiations – their tactics

1 Do note that the Chinese prefer to negotiate in China, which gives them several advantages.
2 Do expect a large Chinese team.
3 Do discount enthusiastic Chinese statements about future prospects and their own power.
4 Do note that foreigners are expected to reveal their position first.
5 Do be aware that the Chinese seek your weaknesses and observe your body-language closely.
6 Do observe that the Chinese stress mutual interests, not compromise, but they think in terms of winners and losers.
7 Do expect major issues to be raised on social occasions.
8 Do expect to be played off against competitors.
9 Do note that time and money are separate concepts in China.
10 Do observe that the Chinese see negotiations differently.
11 Do anticipate that the Chinese will keep returning to and raising old issues.
12 Do expect the Chinese to wander in and out during talks.
13 Do observe that *guanxi* ('pull' with people in a relationship) is much used.
14 Do note the importance of symbols.
15 Do expect the truth to be a flexible commodity.
16 Do expect the Chinese to press for much free information.
17 Do expect to meet rather insensitive single-mindedness on occasion.

Contracts

18 Do note that the attitude towards contracts is different and do not be surprised if you are asked to change a contract.
19 Do be careful with joint venture contract negotiations.
20 When in a joint venture be prepared to face continuous negotiations and suggested contract amendments.

21   Do note the different attitude to law and the preference for conciliation.
22   Do note that internal and secret regulations exist.
23   Do note that politics is still of prime importance in China.
24   Do observe that the Chinese often expect a 'sweetener' to be thrown into the deal.

21 *Socializing and proper behaviour*

1 Do note the importance of banquets, which are held early in the evening.
2 Do observe the strict rules of greeting and seating.
3 Do note the importance of toasting and its etiquette.
4 Do note that table manners are different in China.
5 Do be prepared to discuss Chinese food.
6 Do be prepared to make a gracious speech or even sing.
7 Do leave early after the meal finishes.
8 Do give a return banquet if you went to one and observe the formal etiquette required.

22 How to treat visitors to one's own country

1 Do expect to have to organize your visitors thoroughly.
2 Do meet the Chinese at the airport and see them off.
3 Do let the Chinese live together if they are staying some time.
4 Do entertain in a good Chinese restaurant and observe the necessary etiquette.
5 Do note that they will be pleased to visit your home.

23 Living in China

1 Do note that it is hard to choose a joint venture partner.
2 Do accept that you need a male expat in China if running a joint venture.
3 Do select a suitable person to send.
4 Do ensure that suitable pre-departure training is done, in order to minimize culture shock.
5 Some things to warn a family about.

Establish the ground rules before departure

6 Make clear the company expectations of the manager's role.
7 All must agree on the need to communicate with headquarters.
8 Everyone should be aware of the manager's career path and reassurance should be offered about his position.
9 Training after arrival is required.
10 Do expect that headquarters will worry whose side the expat is on.
11 Coping with the realities of China.

24 Managing joint ventures

1 Do keep your help-mate long enough to learn how to operate.
2 Do try to obtain sufficient management control.
3 Do appreciate that the quality and delivery of materials in China can be a problem; you need freedom to vary the source.
4 Do be careful about initiating changes.
5 Do try not to admit to problems to the Chinese.
6 Do expect large numbers of people to be squashed into rooms.
7 Do expect that product style and fashion will loom low.
8 Do note that costs, some hidden, can be higher than you might expect, and that the infrastructure is weak.

Labour and incentives

9 Do notice the importance of the hierarchy in the firm.
10 Do expect Chinese managers to be reluctant to make decisions and sign documents.
11 Do keep any perks, like banquets, and use them wisely; note the gains from gifts.
12 Do anticipate having to explain in great detail.
13 Do post signs to encourage workers.
14 Do recognize that it may not be easy to discipline workers.
15 Do note that labour-saving is not wanted; expect to have to fight overmanning.
16 Do note that there is no pool of skilled labour.
17 Do note that a boss has social obligations.
18 Do watch for a tendency in a joint venture to stockpile produce.

Part Four
Summary of What Not to Do

25 General points on proper behaviour

1 Do not be surprised at the ambivalent Chinese attitude towards foreigners.
2 Do not assume that there is one type of 'Chinese' or that all Chinese are the same.
3 Do not think that the Chinese are the same as the Japanese.
4 Do not boast or state what should/should not be done.
5 Do not indulge in loud behaviour or hold noisy parties.
6 Do not slump in a chair or put your feet on the table.
7 Do not stand with arms on hips looking down your nose.
8 Do not point with the index finger or indicate directions with the foot or the head.
9 Do not beckon with your finger crooked upwards.
10 Do not be surprised if the Chinese are badly dressed.
11 Do not be surprised to encounter noisy inquisitive women.
12 Do not be surprised to be stared at or pointed out.
13 Do not be surprised if strangers come up to talk to you but do no favours for strangers or change money on the street.
14 Do not assume that laughter means happiness.
15 Do not say 'I hope you are well'.
16 Do not express surprise if you encounter spitting or noisy throat clearing.
17 Do not look askance is shouting or noisy behaviour is encountered.
18 Do not display affection publicly.
19 Do not expect a vast market to make you instant profits.
20 Do not tell jokes, especially political ones.
21 Do not brag about breaking rules or impish behaviour.
22 Do not be surprised if you feel tired but try not to admit it.
23 Do not offer tips, unless one is clearly being demanded.
24 Certain items must *not* be given as gifts.
25 Certain topics must *not* be raised by you or discussed.
26 Do not criticize anything you see or hear.

27   Do not refer to Taiwan as a country or as the 'Republic of China'.
28   Do not simply enter a doorway in front of someone.
29   Do not express surprise if you encounter racist attitudes.
30   Do not be surprised at the poverty or run-down state of buildings.
31   Do not drink the water.
32   Do not ask if someone is a Party member.
33   Do not insist that your group split up to do different things.
34   Do not ever cause someone to lose 'face'.
35   Do not ever touch an abacus you come across.
36   Do not photograph anyone without permission.
37   Do not thoughtlessly ask a private individual to come to your hotel.
38   Do not be surprised if the price you are charged is higher than the locals pay.
39   Do not buy antiques in China unless you are an expert.
40   Do not wear certain colours and combinations of them.

26 Approaching China

1 Do not be surprised if a letter gets no response.
2 Do not send someone too young.
3 Do not send a person with an unsuitable appearance.
4 Do not send anyone who could be heavy-handed, arrogant, impatient, rigid, tense, racist, aloof or loud.
5 Do not send a lone person.
6 Do not change the members of your team if it can be avoided.
7 Do not despair if you keep being asked if yours is the best, even if the nature of the Chinese problem is secret.
8 Do not be afraid of making mistakes.
9 Do not indulge in aggressive or sexy advertising.

27   *Meetings and negotiations*

1   Do not be late for appointments.
2   Do not start trying to negotiate the day you arrive.
3   Do not ignore any member of their team.
4   Do not ever use a Chinese person's given name.
5   Do not sit an Overseas Chinese next to your leader.
6   Do not take the 'honoured seat' unless asked.
7   Do not prune your 'brief introduction' at the start of negotiations.
8   Do not drink too much tea in meetings.
9   Do not assume that the people around you do not speak English.
10   Do not show anxiety or impatience in the early meetings.
11   Do not be pushy or try aggressively to speed up the pace.
12   Do not talk fast or use high-pressure tactics.
13   Do not promise more than you can deliver.
14   Do not say 'no'.
15   Do not think a nod means 'yes'.
16   Do not be surprised if silence greets an awkward question.
17   Do not force a showdown or deliver an ultimatum.
18   Do not reject a preposterous suggestion – discuss it.
19   Do not interrupt anyone.
20   Do not invent a figure off the top of your head or speak off the record.
21   Do not expect quick decisions.
22   Do not be surprised to meet insecurity or uncertainty.
23   Do not show impatience or anger.
24   Do not be surprised to meet anger – it is usually a ploy.
25   Do not be surprised if you are made to feel guilty or are called 'unfriendly'.
26   Do not be surprised if the Chinese refuse things of benefit to them.
27   Do not be surprised if the Chinese keep returning to a topic and discussing it again, including contracts.

28 Do not criticize a Chinese publicly.
29 Do not concede anything too easily.
30 Do not aim to be cosily friendly with the Chinese team.
31 Do not take the 'friendship' remarks too seriously.
32 Do not be alarmed if the Chinese suddenly stop negotiating or suddenly say that they will sign.
33 Do not think that a 'memorandum of understanding', 'letter of intent' or 'protocol' is binding on either party.
34 Do keep your expectations private and do not talk to the press.
35 Do not automatically believe statements that you have a good chance of winning a competitive contract.
36 Do not automatically accept a model contract.
37 Do not worry if you seem to be caught between different government organizations.
38 Do not set your prices too far above international ones.
39 Do not rely on current prices remaining unchanged.
40 Do not talk about prices until you know exactly what is involved.
41 Do not use slang while negotiating.
42 Do not rely solely on a high-level contact.
43 Do not try to establish *guanxi* with very senior people.
44 Do not be surprised if the opposition's negotiating power alters.
45 Do not agree to important matters being put in the appendix of the contract.
46 Do not give expensive gifts, unless one is clearly being requested.
47 Do not spring a surprise to try to gain an advantage.
48 Do not gloat or act like a winner.
49 Do not forget that you need to get profits out of China.
50 Do not hesitate to cut your losses and leave if necessary.

28 Socializing and proper behaviour

1 Do not turn down any invitation to lunch, dinner, etc.
2 Do not expect Chinese wives to be present at a banquet.
3 Do not misuse chopsticks.
4 Do not leave any rice in your personal bowl.
5 Do not lay chopsticks across your bowl at a formal dinner.
6 Do not stick your chopsticks upright in the rice and leave them there.
7 Do not ask for a knife to eat with.
8 Do not look surprised if someone slurps soup or tea.
9 Do not look surprised if someone picks up the bowl to eat from.
10 Do not raise business issues at a banquet.
11 Do not point a teapot spout at anyone.
12 Do not chat in English among yourselves.
13 Do not hang around after dinner or expect entertainment.
14 Do not admire anything in a Chinese home.

29 Living and managing in China

1   Do not send a lone expat to live in China.
2   Do not expect a lot of privacy.
3   Do not jump into a joint venture; consider all the options.
4   Do not agree to an all-Chinese board of management – try for over half.
5   Do not assume that all normal Western facilities will be either needed or available.
6   Do not be surprised to find that you must pay more than state-owned firms for various things.
7   Do not expect your goals and the Chinese ones to be the same.
8   Do not address important officials familiarly.
9   Do not try to establish an egalitarian system.
10 Do not agree to lots of small office cubicles.
11 Do not split the joint venture between cities in any way.
12 Do not expect good quality control.
13 Do not expect that equipment will be properly looked after.
14 Do not expect innovation, lateral thinking, or much creativity.
15 Do not be surprised if good workers are recalled from your joint venture.
16 Do not fire the son or daughter of a powerful local official.
17 Do not get annoyed if 'internal rules' are cited at you.
18 Do not get upset if the bureaucracy does not inform you of something it should.
19 Do not try to introduce a Chinese from one ministry to another.
20 Do not hesitate to 'use the back door' if you need something.

30 How to treat visitors to one's own country

1 Do not serve large steaks and slabs of meat, if entertaining at home.
2 Do not hold barbecues when entertaining.
3 Do not forget to begin the toasting when entertaining in a restaurant.

Index

Advertising, 121, 159
Age, attitudes to, 2, 26, 46, 85, 105, 120, 159
Aircraft, 40, 105
Airports, meeting at, 49, 90, 91, 145, 152
Alcohol, 46, 47, 69, 86, 106, 133
Arrogance, avoiding, 31, 113, 120, 125, 159

Balance of payments, 13
Banquets:
  behaviour at, 46, 84–9, 105, 106, 132, 133, 151, 154
  being careful at, 75, 85–8, 133
  guests at, 89, 132, 162
  importance of, 84, 105, 106, 151, 154
Bicycles, 18, 39, 91, 96, 118, 136
Board of management, 135, 163
Body language, 33, 47, 65, 67, 74, 113, 149
Boisterousness, 37, 111, 112
Brand names, 31, 76, 96, 101
Bureaucracy, 10, 27, 30, 32, 42, 52, 61–3, 66, 67, 79, 95, 104, 125, 137, 138, 148, 163
Bureaucrats and officials, how to treat, 64, 137, 148, 163
Buses, 39
Business cards, 35, 45, 54, 55, 90, 145, 146

CCPIT, 43, 45, 50, 93
Cigarettes, 34, 69, 106, 143
Clapping and applause, 37, 144

Clothing, 18, 33, 34, 96, 113, 114, 143
Colours, vii, 33, 34, 114, 116, 119, 143, 158
Communication, needs and difficulties, x, 48, 51, 57, 62, 97, 99, 129, 153
Communications, 8, 62
Concessions, 67, 71, 74, 75, 83, 125, 130
Confucian values, 15, 18, 19, 25, 29–31, 46, 81, 85, 117, 120, 143
Contracts, 11, 58, 60, 61, 66, 78–81, 83, 102, 104, 111, 124, 127–31, 135, 149, 160, 161
Costs, 66, 75, 95, 104, 105, 125, 127, 131, 148, 154
Culture shock, 34, 35, 41, 72, 94, 116, 135, 153

Delays, 32, 41, 52, 61, 62, 70, 106
Details, 43, 47, 51–3, 57–9, 67, 74, 76, 79, 94, 103, 106, 125, 127, 130, 146, 154
Drinks, 53, 56, 118, 123, 146, 158, 160
  alcoholic, 46, 47, 69, 74, 86

Early meetings, 52–6
Electricity, 62, 80, 102, 104, 136
Employment, 2, 16, 17, 102
English, use of, 51, 57, 69, 79, 89, 97, 98, 114, 123, 132, 133, 145, 160, 162
English language materials, 41, 44, 45, 69, 79
Equipment, 98, 102, 103, 137, 163
  quality of, 6, 39, 42

Experience:
  need for, x, 26, 43, 45, 46, 67, 94,
    95
  shortage of, 12, 67, 104, 107
Eye contact, 33, 143

Face, importance of, 31, 39, 40, 46, 48,
    52, 55, 57, 58, 64, 65, 74, 77, 78,
    84, 89, 90, 104–6, 118, 123–7,
    130, 138, 148, 158
Families, 15, 16, 18, 26, 95
Family, importance of, 11, 15, 18,
    25–30, 41, 48, 112, 137, 143
Fax, 38, 48, 99
Flexibility, need for, 46, 94, 120
Flowers, 116
Food:
  as conversation topic, 40, 41, 54, 69,
    88, 151
  and eating, 85–8, 92, 101, 104, 106,
    132, 133, 139
Foreign investment, 2, 6, 7, 11–14, 17
Foreign trade, 2, 6, 7, 13
Foreigners:
  attitude to, vii, 16, 19, 31, 36–8, 63,
    71, 78, 79, 81, 85, 87, 94, 111,
    112, 114, 115, 116, 117, 121,
    123, 126, 144, 157
  treatment of, 11, 14, 18, 40, 45, 64,
    69, 78, 97, 105, 115, 119, 127,
    149
Frustrations, 27, 41, 42, 48, 95, 101,
    126, 144

GATT, 7, 8, 11
General principles, beginning with, 58,
    59, 77, 80, 147
Gifts, 48, 68, 69, 83, 106, 116, 131,
    154
  item suitability, 68, 69, 116, 130,
    148, 157, 161
Go-between, 67, 102, 103, 125, 148,
    see also Help-mate; Intermediary
Group, importance of, 18, 25, 27–30,
    64, 81, 82, 112, 117, 118, 135,
    158
Guanxi, 43, 51, 62, 76, 130, 149, 161
Guilt, feelings of, 57, 74, 126, 160

Harmony, 18, 25, 27, 30, 31, 41, 47,
    88, 124, 125, 143
Health, 34, 97
Help-mate, 44, 50, 73, 107, 145, *see
    also* Go-between; Intermediary
Hierarchy, 27, 29, 30, 46, 49, 53, 55,
    90, 105, 120, 130, 139, 143, 154
Homes, visiting, 68, 69, 84, 92, 103,
    116, 134, 162
Honesty, 63, 64, 77, 148
Hong Kong, 2, 7, 11, 13, 21, 34, 45,
    92, 97–9, 119, 131, 143
Host, behaviour of, 49–51, 53, 54, 69,
    71, 72, 84–9, 91, 100, 123, 134,
    139
Host unit, 40, 50, 51, 54, 61, 84, 146
Hotels, 21, 27, 32, 35, 38, 41, 45, 50,
    51, 53, 69, 70, 91, 96, 97, 101,
    105, 113, 114, 116, 118, 119, 133,
    135, 144, 158
  in your country, 90–2
Humour, 29, 116, *see also* Jokes

Impatience, 56, 62, 74, 120, 124, 126,
    159, 160
Incentives, 10, 105, 106, 154
Inflation, 5, 12, 13, 14
Informality in approach, 52, 122, 139,
    146
Infrastructure, 11, 16, 101, 104, 112, 154
Initial contacts, 43–5, 145
Insiders, concept of, 29, 38, 39, 51, 62,
    70, 120, 125, 137, 143
Intermediary, 44, 65, 125, *see also* Go-
    between; Help-mate
Interpreters, 48, 51, 53, 57, 58, 61, 68,
    85, 88–90, 122, 123, 125, 147
  bringing your own, 47, 51, 57, 58,
    123, 147
Invitations, issuing, 69, 70, 72, 88, 89,
    106, 148

Japanese, similarities and differences,
    29, 31, 33, 46, 77, 94, 111, 112,
    157
Joint ventures, v, vi, viii, 10, 16, 48,
    75, 80, 81, 91, 93, 102, 104,
    105–8, 135–7, 149, 153, 154, 163

Jokes, 41, 88, 116, 157

Koreans, differences and similarities, 31, 33, 37

Labour, v, vi, 8, 10, 14, 17, 75, 105, 107, 112, 154
  and costs, 2, 75
Laughter, 29, 114, 115, 157
Law, attitude towards, 15, 59, 79–82, 150
Laws, 29, 77, 82
Leader:
  of Chinese team, 45, 53–5, 58, 61, 64, 72, 73, 88–90, 122, 126, 131, 143, 146
  of your team, 29, 45, 46, 53–5, 85, 90, 120, 122, 143, 160
Leadership of China, 1, 3–5, 9, 12, 13, 19, 29, 36, 41, 55, 116, 117
Legal situation, 3, 10, 16, 57, 58, 79–82, 93, 107
Letters, 44, 48, 58, 65, 98, 107, 114, 120, 135, 143, 159, 161
  Chinese attitude towards, 30, 44, 48, 65, 120, 143, 159
Letters of intent, 58, 128, 161
Long-term relationship, 46, 61, 67, 111, 112, 131
Lunch, 34, 35, 55, 90, 104, 132, 143, 146, 162

Macao, 7, 11
Manners:
  bad, 33, 36, 37, 48, 87, 112, 113, 127, 131, 133
  good, vii, ix, 31, 36, 37, 63, 69, 77, 84, 86, 87, 143
Mao Zedong, 2, 3, 8, 9, 20, 27, 34, 63, 67, 103, 117
Maoism, 3–6, 17, 18, 28, 30, 77, 82, 113, 114
Mature people, respect for, 2, 46, 94, 120
Medicine, 34, 41, 97, 143
Meetings, 35, 37, 47, 48, 52–6, 61–3, 65, 66, 73–5, 79, 116, 123, 124, 130, 131, 133, 146, 148, 149, 160
Memorandum of understanding, 58, 128, 161

Moustaches and wavy hair, 120

Names, 27, 29, 35, 39, 43, 52–4, 57, 90, 106, 122, 143, 145, 146, 160
Nepotism, 107, 137
'No':
  avoid saying, 67, 78, 124, 125, 160
  recognizing, 30, 65, 148
Notes, value of taking, 53, 56, 66, 73, 79, 147
Numbers, ix, 3, 17, 32, 38, 58, 72, 89, 103, 135, 143, 154

'Old friends', 31, 61, 70, 71, 77, 120
Organizations, 14, 27, 29, 39, 40, 49–52, 54, 59, 76, 82, 83, 125, 129, 145, 146, 161
Outsiders, 29, 30, 38, 51, 62, 70, 82, 121, 125, 129, 137, 138, 143
Overseas Chinese, 11, 26, 47, 48, 51, 57, 64, 69, 119, 122, 123, 145, 160

Patience, need for, 46, 63, 94, 105, 125, 137
Patriotism, strength of, 28, 117, 143
Perks, importance of, 105, 106, 154
Persistence, 59, 63, 69, 79, 126, 136, 148
Politeness:
  forms of, 31, 35, 45, 54, 63, 65, 69, 71, 85, 87, 100, 103, 128
  need for, vii, 63, 78, 85, 106, 122, 130, 148
Political changes, 2–7, 9, 15, 19, 82, 95
Politics, discussing, 41, 116, 117, 126, 157
Prestige, preference for, 30, 31, 76, 143
Prices:
  in China, 9, 10, 13, 27, 29, 78–81, 91, 95, 97, 105, 119, 129, 131, 158, 161
  setting yours, 66, 73, 79, 80, 83, 125, 129, 148, 161

Profits:
  for the Chinese, 14, 59, 74, 136
  for foreigners, 36, 43, 59, 66-8, 81,
    99, 116, 131, 136, 157, 161
Protocol, 53, 54, 89, 128, 146, 161
Punctuality, 51, 122, 146

Quality:
  attitudes to, 103, 106, 112, 136,
    163
  of goods and materials, 27, 34, 81,
    96, 97, 101, 102, 104, 137, 154
  of labour force, 16, 75, 104, 105,
    137
  Questions you might face, 40, 41, 46,
    47, 57, 66, 121, 144

Racism, 112, 117, 120, 158, 159
Ranks and hierarchy, 30, 32, 45, 49,
  90, 91, 130, 143
Raw materials, 9, 50, 81, 102, 104,
  108, 129, 136, 137, 154
Repeat yourself and summarize, 51, 66,
  148
Restaurants, 41, 69, 84, 87-9, 92, 96,
  132, 133, 139, 144, 152, 164
Rivalry, of areas, firms or products, 61,
  62, 72, 136, 148
Rudeness, 30, 31, 51, 55, 63, 76, 86,
  98, 112, 116, 122, 127, 148

Safe topics, 41, 66, 85, 144
Samples, 78, 121
Seating, 29, 39, 40, 53, 54, 84, 85, 89,
  92, 113, 123, 139, 151, 160
Secrecy, 8, 16, 38, 67, 71, 82, 118,
  121, 137, 144, 150, 159
Seniority, 26, 46, 71, 84, 89, 91, 120,
  122, 130, 148, 161
SEZs, *see* Special Economic Zones
Shame, use of, 59, 74, 126
Silence, use and meaning of, 65, 73, 74,
  86, 124, 160
Singapore, 2, 19, 31
Smiling, 31, 33, 38, 45, 53, 55, 69, 76,
  87, 88, 127, 143
Soft approaches, 48, 63, 145

Special Economic Zones, 9, 11-13, 50,
  93, 107
Standing close, 33, 143
Status, 2, 16, 30, 46, 47, 49, 50, 70,
  71, 79, 82, 84, 123, 146
Stock markets, 9
Superstition, 18, 32, 33, 133, 143
Symbolism, 43, 55, 76, 77, 86, 104,
  116, 133, 149

Taiwan, 2, 6-8, 16, 44, 86, 102, 116,
  117, 158
Taxation, 14, 16, 104, 106
Tea, vii, 56, 87, 123, 133, 146, 160,
  162
Team:
  theirs, 26, 27, 45, 55, 57, 64, 67, 68,
    72, 73, 86, 122, 127, 131, 133,
    135, 149, 160, 161
  yours, 29, 45-8, 53, 55, 57, 68, 76,
    88, 89, 120, 123, 145, 159
Technology, 30-2, 77, 112, 113, 121,
  148
Technology, foreign, 2, 11, 30-2, 36,
  44, 47, 54, 61, 68, 73, 76, 113,
  121, 148
Telephones, 27, 35, 38, 48, 80, 99,
  104, 119, 136, 144
Tipping, 70, 116, 157
Tiredness, 35, 46, 55, 62, 63, 72, 113,
  116, 122, 135, 143, 148, 157
Toasting, 47, 86, 139, 151, 164
Traditional values, ix, 18, 20, 26, 27,
  30, 32, 33, 45, 46, 59, 62, 75, 77,
  82, 85, 86, 93, 112, 113, 115,
  117, 119, 120, 126, 132
Traffic, 39, 91, 144
Training worker, 54, 66, 72, 77, 83,
  91, 93-5, 99, 100, 103-5, 107,
  129, 135, 136, 137, 153
Trains, 40, 105
Transport, 8, 16, 39, 91, 102, 118, 144
Trust, 2, 20, 33, 36, 37, 53, 54, 56,
  65, 100, 120, 121, 127, 129
Truth, 63-5, 77, 81, 148, 149

Ultimata, dangers of issuing, 124, 125,
  160

Unemployment, 10, 14, 107
Unsafe topics, 41, 85, 116, 117, 144, 157

Wages, 10, 75, 104, 106, 107
Waiting around, 35, 40, 41, 51, 53, 66, 144
Water, 8, 80, 101, 104, 118, 136, 158
Weakness, Chinese probe for, 56, 74, 126, 149

Who to send, 30, 45–7, 70, 71, 93, 94, 120, 135, 145, 148, 153, 159, 163
Wives, 69, 94, 95, 99, 115, 132, 162
Women, 34, 35, 101, 117, 132, 157
    attitude towards, 29, 35, 39, 46, 93, 105, 114
Women's clothing, 34, 85

'Yes', misinterpreting, 124, 160
Younger generation, ix, 39, 85, 114, 115

KAT - No question about whether to go upshore . True?
New issues
upbeat on India / China

names of a couple people & their coach who gives p.s.
Security issues - what does she do?
why does she feel comfortable

gestures - small fingers, feet
words - love

x p. 8 sacred, unchanging

x demand caution

x TALK w. Liz
see videos

x selective curity